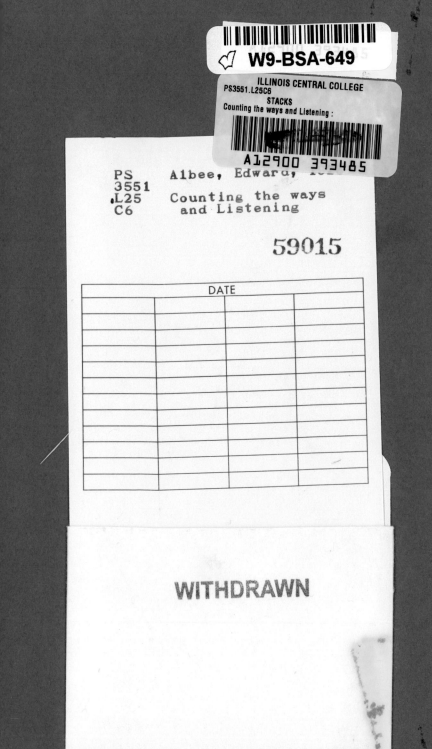

DATE			

PLAYS BY

EDWARD ALBEE

(DATES OF COMPOSITION)

COUNTING THE WAYS	1976
LISTENING	1975
SEASCAPE	1975
ALL OVER	1971
BOX AND QUOTATIONS	
FROM CHAIRMAN MAO TSE-TUNG	1968
A DELICATE BALANCE	1966
TINY ALICE	1964
WHO'S AFRAID OF VIRGINA WOOLF?	1961–1962
THE AMERICAN DREAM	1960
THE SANDBOX	1959
THE DEATH OF BESSIE SMITH	1959
THE ZOO STORY	1958

ADAPTATIONS

EVERYTHING IN THE GARDEN	1967
(from the play by Giles Cooper)	
MALCOLM	1965
(from the novel by James Purdy)	
THE BALLAD OF THE SAD CAFE	1963
(from the novella by Carson McCullers)	

COUNTING THE WAYS

AND

LISTENING

EDWARD ALBEE

, 1928 -

COUNTING
THE
WAYS

A N D

LISTENING

TWO PLAYS

NEW YORK 1977

ATHENEUM

Library of Congress Cataloging in Publication Data

Albee, Edward, 1928–
    Counting the ways and Listening.

    I. Title.
PS3551.L25C6   812'.5'4   76-52438
ISBN 0-689-10785-4

FOR

BILL & WILLY
WILLY & BILL

COUNTING
THE
WAYS

(*A Vaudeville*)

1976

THE SET

I see a fairly short rear wall, and two side walls angling from it to the proscenium. In each of the side walls I see an archway cut, for entrances and exits. Beyond these archways we see black. On stage, there should be a round, or oval table, three feet diameter, dining-table height. To either side of the table there should be a straightback armless chair. The walls bare: on the table: a magazine, a pipe, and whatever else may be needed. No clutter, though!

LIGHTS

Clear, white light; the only shift is the fade at the end of the play. (See: BLACKOUTS for further notes)

COSTUMES AND MAKEUP

Both of these simple and naturalistic.

BLACKOUTS

This is more a term than a method, though I would like the lights to go out at once, and come on as suddenly, when called for. If need be, a curtain could be swiftly drawn and as swiftly opened.

THE SIGNS

Exactly as described. If coming from above is a problem, they may appear on a signboard, far stage right, in the old vaudeville manner—placed there by a disembodied hand.

COUNTING THE WAYS *received its first American performance at The Hartford Stage Co., January 28, 1977*

SHE *Angela Lansbury*

HE *William Prince*

Directed by EDWARD ALBEE

AVANT SCENE

The stage empty.

A sign drops:
COUNTING THE WAYS.
Stays four seconds, rises.

BLACKOUT

SCENE ONE

The TWO *reading.*

SHE
(Puts her magazine down, looks at him for a little while, HE *reads, smokes his pipe. Objective curiosity)*
Do you *love* me?

HE
(Takes a while to register that HE *has been asked a question)*
Hm? Pardon?

SHE
(*Even more emphasis on the word "love"*)
Do you *love* me?

HE
(*Considers it for quite a while; suspicious*)
Why do you ask?

SHE (*Considers that*)
Well: because I want to know.

HE (*Pause; puzzled*)
Right *now*?

SHE (*Suddenly uncertain*)
Well . . . *yes*. Or . . . no, no, not really.
(*Short pause*)
Yes.

HE
(*Considers it, finds the question silly, shows it*)
Of course.

SHE (*"Good for you!"*)
Well . . . good.
(SHE *smiles, goes back to her book.* HE *looks at her for a moment, goes back to his*)

BLACKOUT

SCENE TWO

*THEY both have moved to standing positions, each
to one side of the stage, near their exitways.*

SHE (*Bright, but not idiotic*)

Walnuts!

(*This is a list; small expectant pauses*)

Parsley!
Bone marrow!
Celery root!
Crème brulée!

(*Pause; enthusiastic*)

Do you love me?!

HE (*Hungry and delighted*)

Of course!

SHE (*"Right on!"*)

I *knew* you did!

(*THEY both exit*)

BLACKOUT

SCENE THREE

Stage empty; SHE *reappears, bitter and resentful;*
SHE *crosses toward his exitway, talks toward it.*

SHE

Do you suppose stuffing it in me for you fat and flabby is
something I enjoy? Do you? Putting it in me like a wad of

dough . . . hoping it'll "rise" to the occasion? Do you think that fills me with a sense of . . . what? Fills me with anything but itself? There are deserts, you know! And think about hence!!

(*Pause*)

There are two things: cease and corruption. And that's all there is to say about hence!

(*Pause*)

Except, perhaps, that predetermination is even more awful than . . . what do they call it?—"the sudden void"? There's that, too.

(*Pause; grim assurance*)

One day . . . one day stuffing it in me for you—fat and flabby, yes, fat and flabby—it will *not*, in its own good time, "rise" to the occasion, and nevermore, as the bird said. When *that* day comes . . . well, that day comes.

(*Short pause*)

And knowing all that, what do you call now!?

(*Short pause*)

You call it love!

(*Longer pause; more determined*)

You call it love! Remember it!

(SHE *exits, her exitway*)

BLACKOUT

SCENE FOUR

Stage empty; HE *enters, holding a newspaper open to where* HE *has been reading;* HE *has his reading glasses on;* HE *assumes* SHE *is in the room.*

HE (*Reads from his paper*)

"Love in the afternoon."

(*Sees* HE *is alone; calls*)

"Love in the afternoon." What does that *mean*?

(*Pause*)

Where *are* you?

SHE

(*Enters, carrying a plate and dishcloth*)

What? Love in the what?

HE

"Love in the afternoon," it says; that's a title. What does it mean?

SHE (*Considers it*)

"Love in the afternoon"? It means *sex* in the afternoon, I should imagine.

HE (*Mildly incredulous*)

Really? That's what they *mean*? *Sex* in the afternoon? Love means sex? I mean, to *them*?

SHE

Sure: love means sex; eyes are thighs; lips means hips. I kiss your lips means . . .

HE (*The incredulity less mild*)

. . . I kiss your *hips*? I kiss your lips means I kiss your hips?

SHE

Sure.

HE

No.

SHE (*Shrugs*)

I don't care.

HE (*More emphasis*)

I kiss your *hips!?* Nobody ever said that: "Hello, I want to kiss your hips."

SHE (*Laughs*)

I rather like it!

HE (*Dogmatic*)

Nobody ever *said* that.

SHE

Still . . . it's what it means.

HE

And the limpid pools of your eyes? Is that meant to be thighs? The limpid pools of your thighs?

SHE (*Some distaste*)

Don't be literal.

HE

The limpid pools of your thighs?
(*Offhand*)
I don't believe it.

SHE (*Also*)

Call 'em up; find out.

HE (*Taking the dare*)

I will! "Love in the afternoon." I'll just *do* that.

SHE (*A chuckle*)
Good! You do that!
(THEY *both exit*)

BLACKOUT

SCENE FIVE

Stage empty. SHE *enters, still carrying her plate and towel.* SHE *comes center stage, looks at the audience.*

SHE
(*Objective; maybe a bit too bright*)
Here's a thought; I think it was my grandmother's: *love* doesn't die; we pass *through* it.
(SHE *stares at the audience for a little, without emotion, looks at the plate in her hand, exits*)

SCENE SIX

SHE *is center, putting a rose in a vase;* HE *enters.*

HE
You're right.

SHE
Hm? Pardon?

HE

You're right. I went there and I asked them. "Love in the afternoon" means sex. Sex in the afternoon.

SHE

Well, of course; I told you.

HE (*A little hurt*)

I was surprised.

SHE (*Busy*)

Did you ask about eyes and thighs and lips and hips?

HE

No; I was embarrassed.
(*Pause*)
Love in the morning means sex in the morning, too.

SHE

Oh, you asked about that.

HE

Yes; they smiled; smirked.

SHE (*A trifle tart*)

And love at night?

HE

I didn't ask.

SHE
(*Starts slow, offhand, builds*)

Love at night? After all the drinks? And too much food? The old arguments hashed over for the guests? The car? That week in Bermuda? The nursing home? All that? The bile and

the regrets and half numb and better off straight to sleep but no, fumbling and a little hatred with each thrust—both ways?
(*Laughs*)
Oh my; love in the afternoon may be one thing, and love in the morning very much the same, they may both be dirty games, but love at night . . . oh, that has to be love.
(*Long pause*)

HE (*Embarrassed*)

They smirked.

SHE (*Right at him*)

Did they.
(*Pause; a little too offhand*)
What time is it?

BLACKOUT

SCENE SEVEN

SHE *has exited;* HE *is alone with the rose in the vase.* HE *circles it, looks to see if* SHE *is coming, looks at the rose, takes it from the vase and begins to de-petal it.*

HE

She loves me.
She loves me not.
(*Etc., for maybe 25–30 petals, varying in speed, varying in mood, but with no imposed psychological progression*)

She loves me.

She loves me not.

>(HE *becomes aware of the audience and cups the remainder of the rose from view; now* HE *feels conspicuous*)

She loves me.

She loves me not.

>(HE *peers into his hand at the cupped rose, looks very seriously at the audience, and then suddenly pops the remainder of the flower into his mouth, chews, pretends to swallow.* HE *holds up the stem;* HE *smiles*)

BLACKOUT

SCENE EIGHT

HE *is sitting; the stem is in the vase;* SHE *enters.*

SHE

(*Comes to the table for something, sees the stem*)
What's this!?

>(SHE *picks up the stem*)

HE (*Looking up*)

What?

SHE

This. What happened?

HE

I ate it.

SHE

The rose?

HE

The flower.

SHE

What for?

HE (*Calm; a trifle confused*)

Well . . . I took the rose and I was doing the petals for she-loves-me-she-loves-me-not . . .

SHE (*Points to the table top*)

Yes, I can see.

HE (*Looks*)

Oh; there they *are*. And I was counting away—very interested —and I was nearing a decision—she-loves-me-she-loves-me-not . . .

SHE

Who?

HE

You, of course. And I was near a verdict . . .

SHE (*None too friendly*)

Why didn't you just *ask* me?

HE (*Slow and determined*)

Well, I had already begun with the *rose*, and it was here and you were not . . .

SHE (*Sniffs*)

You should have asked *me*.

HE

. . . and it was going along quite nicely . . .

SHE

I would have told you.

HE

. . . one way, then the other, when all at once I saw I was being watched . . .
      (*Waits to see if* SHE *will react;* SHE *doesn't*)
. . . out *there.*
                              (*Ibid*)
. . . out *there!*
      (*Points;* SHE *looks, accepts, turns back to him, nods*)

HE

. . . and so . . .

SHE

. . . so?

HE (*Deflated*)

. . . and so I ate it—what was left.

SHE (*Triumphant*)

You just didn't want to know!

HE (*Holding his own*)

They were *watching!*

SHE

Ask *me! I'll* tell you!

HE (*Pause; moves to exit*)

I'll get another rose.

SHE

Ask *me!* I'll *tell* you!

HE

I'll get another one.

(*Exits*)

SHE (*Pause; calls after him*)
You'll get *sick.* You can't eat *roses!* You'll get *sick!*

BLACKOUT

SCENE NINE

SHE *is alone on stage.* SHE *looks at the stem in her
hand, looks down at the petals on the table, looks
toward his exit, back. Taking the opportunity of being alone—but still furtively—*SHE *picks up the petals
one by one and relates them to the stem.*

SHE

He loves me?
He loves me not?
No; that's not right; that's when you take them off.
Not me loves he?
Me loves he?
Not me loves he?
Me loves he? (Etc.)
    (SHE *does this for not more than 30 seconds, as little
    as 10, at the discretion of the director.* SHE *will vary
    in mood and intensity—enthusiasm, dismay, surety,*

*uncertainty, anger, pleasure—but by the end of the
mood will be some confusion and bitterness*)
Not me loves he?
Me loves he?
      (HE *enters, carrying a new rose, the other hand be-
      hind his back*)

                              H E
              (*Puzzled and faintly superior*)
What are you doing? Aren't you silly! Here's a new one.
What were you doing?
      (SHE *looks at him, then at his rose, then at her stem.*
      SHE *puts her stem down on the table, takes his rose
      with a swipe of her hand, exits.*
      HE *stands for a moment, looking after her*)

                    B L A C K O U T

                    S C E N E   T E N

      As at the end of the previous scene. HE *turns toward
      the audience, brings his hand from behind his back;*
      HE *is holding another rose.* HE *smiles gently, looks
      at it, smells it.*

                              H E (*To himself, more or less*)
Maybe it was the daisies.
              (*Now to the audience*)
Maybe it was daisies.
                    (*Pause*)
After all, I mean. Maybe you can't *do* it with roses. Well . . .
maybe you can't do it with daisies, either. Daisies tell? Daisies

do *what*? What did we do with dandelions? In the fall, when we were young, when the yellow was gone and they were ready to blow . . . so . . . fragile, regular showoffs. Dandelion?* Lion's tooth? For all that fluff? Must have been the leaves. All that fluff. One blew them for a reason. What was it? In the fall, when we were young. Was it for love? I mean, was it a way of telling?

(*Pause*)

I could look it up. I *could*; I probably *will*, but not knowing anymore—having known, of course, *aware* of that, and longer —there's a kind of shivery thing there. There's something thrilling to the mind going. As with deafness—all the encroachments. Or can less encroach?

(*Small pause*)

Slow falling apart; it's interesting. Well, it had better be!

(*Pause*)

What did we use them for? We blew them for a reason when we were young. What was it? Was it for love?

(*Louder, so* SHE *will hear, offstage*)

Was it for love?

SHE (*Offstage*)

Hm? Pardon?

HE

(*A little louder; over his shoulder*)

Was it for love? Did we blow them for love?

(HE *sees her stick her head in; softer*)

Was it for love?

SHE

I'm sorry I grabbed it like that.

(*Hands it*)

Do you want it back?

* French pronunciation.

HE (*Doesn't take it*)
I mean dandelions, after all, I think; not roses.

SHE

What?

HE

Not roses any longer; probably never; dandelions. I don't *mean* roses anymore.

SHE (*Pause; thinks for a bit*)
We shouldn't each have a rose like this; they should be together; one of us should have both of them.

HE
(*Pause; a slight, superior laugh*)
What will you do, make an arrangement?

SHE
(*Pauses momentarily; snaps*)
Never mind.
(*Exits with her rose*)

HE (*Looks after her; pause*)
I *think* it was for love; it was a long time ago.
(HE *looks at his rose, holds it at stiff arm's length toward her exit, closes his eyes tight*)
Here.

BLACKOUT

SCENE ELEVEN

As at the end of the previous scene. Eyes still closed,
HE *makes a grimace, extends, shakes his flower-held*
arm even further.

HE *(Between-the-teeth tone)*

HERE!

(Nothing happens)

BLACKOUT

SCENE TWELVE

As before.

HE

Here!
(SHE *enters, with rose, pauses, sighs, takes the rose*)
I mean! . . . really!

(HE *exits*)

SHE *(After him)*

Well, you see . . .
(*Stops, considers the roses; speaks to the audience*
now; begins brightly)
There was another time I had them like this—two of them;
two flowers! Not in my hand, though, but two. I was what!?
I was seventeen and seventeen was younger, then.
(*A confidence*)
Some of us—believe it; try to believe it—some of us at seven-

teen were, oh, shame, I suppose, to present eyes, still maidens, still maidens, head and hood.

(Considers that)

Hm! And I was at a dance, and we all wore satin then and looked very much alike—not from the satin, not only that, but our hair was of a style, and our skin—what was it? Was it something we used, or was it seventeen?—our skin was glistening and palest pink—save when we blushed, which was deep and often—the palest pink, and we all had a bit of . . . pudge. That's a nice way to put it, I think: a bit of pudge. I had come, I think, with the boy my mother said I should, and that didn't matter, for one was like another. I think I was *sixteen*. One was like another: one bit his nails; one wore brown shoes, dirty brown shoes with his tux; another . . . these roses will wilt. Ah, well.

One was like another and it didn't matter. The music was . . . well, it was a prom.

The boy had bought me a gardenia, a flower I have always, perhaps irrationally, loathed—nowadays their scent makes me faintly ill; the gardenia; a corsage; not a wristlet, alas, for I could have kept it some distance *from* me, but a corsage which, he asked, could he *place* on me.

Well, it was a chance for a feel, though God knows what they got, those bras our mothers had us wear, but the boys *I* knew weren't too adventuresome—lots of blowing in the ear, nibbles, a creeping hand in the dark once or twice; nothing much. I *must* have been sixteen.

HE *(Appearing stage right)*

Where are my shirts?

SHE

(Hears, pays no attention; still to the audience)

Well, he put it on me—placed, as he said—above my left breast, and a little low, sort of . . . *on* it rather than above it.

(*Demonstrates with the flower in her left hand;
keeps it in place*)

HE (*Moving right of center*)

I want my shirts!

SHE (*As before*)

I kept my head to the right a lot, but there's no avoiding a
gardenia once it gets the body heat. Suddenly . . . suddenly
there was another boy at our table, standing there, looking
down at me with a sort of . . . puzzled hurt.

HE

(*Moving left of center; a whine*)

Where are my shirts?

SHE (*As before*)

I couldn't place him at once. He was from school; I couldn't
place *that*, and then the water cooler sprang to my mind!

HE (*Left of center; louder*)

I want my shirts!

SHE

(*Vague intimation of having heard him but still to
the audience; some wonder*)

The water cooler, and the image of *that* boy . . . he was a
loner, or new, or no one liked him: a cabal, perhaps—a week
or so previous, I had stopped by the cooler—though tepid as
often as not—and coming back up from my drink, I *sensed*
him . . . or, who he proved to be, rather as I suddenly sensed
him at our table. I remember, he said . . .

HE

Why don't I have any shirts?

SHE (*Right on*)

. . . are you going to the prom? Not inviting me, it is important to remember, but . . . asking. Sure, I said, nodding my head, swallowing; quiet smile; you? He nodded. I walked away. See you! I said. Maybe *that* was it! "See you!" Could he have? . . . he *must* have!

HE

Everyone has *shirts*. Why don't *I* have any?

SHE (*Pays no attention*)

Does "See you" mean something more? Does "See you" mean "I suspect you're inviting me, subtly, of course, and naturally I accept."? Does "See you" mean *that*? It *must!*

HE

I must have *shirts*. Where are my *shirts?*

SHE (*As just before*)

He was so shy. "I'm late," he said; "here." And from behind his back he brought a gardenia corsage, twin to the one I already had. Everyone sensed the error, the gaffe, the poor boy's . . . the misunderstanding. There was no need for my date, whoever he was, to be so rude, so . . . cruel and . . . "Well, hey, can I pin 'er?" "Sure; sure! Pin 'er. Pin 'er and scram!"

HE

Thousands have lived without love, but none without shirts.

SHE (*Teacherlike*)

The numbing inevitability of dream!
(*Back to chatty tone*)

There was only one breast left, of course, and the right one at that, and he sought it out! He stood off, measured the mark, and pinned me on the right, twin to the left.

(*Let her demonstrate this*)

"Now, scram!" And scram he did, if one can do it slowly; well, he went, with a little smile and a wink which touches me deeply as I think of it now. It did not, then, for there I was, both breasts aflower and no direction to turn my head.

(*Pause;* SHE *gazes at the roses*)

These will wilt!

(*An afterthought; a smile*)

No, I didn't marry him—the shy boy—either one, for that matter.

(*Offhand*)

I never saw the shy boy again. I have thought about him, though, from time to time, during love.

BLACKOUT

SCENE THIRTEEN

HE *alone on stage, holding the flowers.*

HE (*Chuckling*)

Did you hear what I said? I thought it was rather good. "Thousands have lived without love . . ."

SHE

(*Swats him with the roses; urgently, vaguely accusatory*)

These will wilt!

(SHE *exits*)

HE

(*Looks at the flowers; accepting but uninvolved*)
Wilt they will.
(*Puts his arm down; the heads of the flowers face
the floor. To the audience*)
I thought that was rather good, there, before, what I said:
"Thousands have lived without love, but none without
shirts." I did; I thought it was quite good.
(*Tosses it off*)
What does *she* know?
(*As before*)
It's a parody, of course. You *knew* that; *some* of you knew
that. It's W. H. Auden. "Thousands have lived without love,
but none without water" . . . is the line. What's it from?
. . . "In Praise of Limestone"? Probably. *Something* in the
middle there. You can do it with most anything:
Walnuts.
Parsley.
Bone marrow.
Celery root.
Crème Brulée.
"Thousands have lived without love, but none without Crème
Brulée."
You see? It works.
It lacks . . . well, it doesn't . . . there's not as much *reso-
nance* that way . . . Crème Brulée for water, or *shirts* for
water, for that matter, but if parody *isn't* a diminishment
. . . well, then, was it worth it in the first place?
(*Thinks*)
Auden was one of the ones I cried when he died. Did I *cry*?
Well, something. Something . . . *left* me, at any rate.
If you can get *away*, if you can *watch* your emotions, you
know that pain is a misunderstanding: it's really *loss*; *loss* is
what it's *really* about.

(*Looks at the flowers; objective tone*)
When will they wilt?
(*Lowers them again; to the audience again*)
Oh . . . there *is* the breathtaker, that sudden sharp sense,
but that's the *brain* . . . panicking, sending out contradictory
impulses: not enough oxygen, and the host can faint, you
know? And that heart attack at shocking news? It's just the
head saying, "That's enough! I've had enough; I don't want
any more; let's quit all this . . . what do you call it? Life?"
But most of it's not that *way*. Most of it's slow and after the
fact and has to do with going on *without* something, something we thought was necessary—essential—but then discov-
ered it merely made all the difference: one *could* go on if
one really *wanted* to.
(*Considers*)
Three times, I think, in long pants; crying: Auden; a cat, a
very old cat; and something to do with civilization.
(*Pause*)
I suppose one selects.
(*Pause*)

SHE
(*Pokes her head in; curiously excited*)
They're going to wilt!
They're going to wilt!

HE (*Preoccupied; at a loss*)
Yes; well, bring a vase.

SHE (*Eager*)
No, they should be on the table . . . between our beds!
(SHE *exits whence* SHE *entered*)

HE
(*Long pause as that sinks in. Exits after her, be-
wildered*)

When did *that* happen?
When did *that* happen!?

(Exits)

BLACKOUT

SCENE FOURTEEN

Stage empty; THEY *re-enter,* SHE *first,* HE *urgently following after.*

SHE

I don't want to discuss it!

HE (Persisting)

When did it happen!?

SHE

I do *not* wish to *discuss* it!

HE

Well, I *do.*

SHE
(Smiles a small, superior smile)

Then, we are at an impasse.

(Fr. pronunciation)

HE

No, we are not; we will discuss it.

SHE (*Didactic*)

If I will not, and only you will, that is not a discussion.

HE (HE, *too*)

Silence is a reply.

SHE (*Snorts*)

Of sorts. For some, I suppose. Martyrs in the desert? Old people at the post office?

HE (*Stern*)

When did it happen?

SHE (*Transparent*)

What? I have no idea what.

HE

Two beds.

SHE (*Ibid*)

So?

HE (*Voice rising*)

There are two beds!

SHE (*Straining to remain calm*)

Yes; there are two beds.

HE (*Suddenly; loud, hysterical*)

WHY!!??

SHE (*Overly calm*)

Well; let us sit down and discuss it.

(SHE *sits*)

With calm and reason.

HE
(*Bolts down into the other chair; urgent if softer*)
O.K.! Right! O.K.!

SHE

Greater calm.

HE (*Softer, but still urgent*)
O.K. Right. O.K.

SHE

And reason.

HE
(*Some reason, but still aquiver*)
Reason? Sure! All of a sudden there are two beds. Once upon a time there was one.

SHE (*Grudging*)
I . . . I *noticed* that.

HE
I wake up this morning . . . in our king-size bed . . .

SHE
You've moved into the historical present, I hope you realize.

HE
(*Tries to ignore her; voice tenser*)
I wake up this morning in our king-size bed . . .

SHE (*To the audience*)
It's an odd tense, isn't it—sort of common, if you know what I mean. It's useful, I know, but . . . *still.*

HE

I won't be put *off*.

SHE
(Back to him, reassuring, not patronizing)
No, no; of course not!

HE

I wake up this morning in our king-size bed, the one I've
waked in every day for seven years . . .

SHE

. . . six . . .

HE

. . . and so have *you*—save trips and hospitals—the bed I
can reach across and touch you in the dark . . . in the
night . . .

SHE
(The slightest tinge of impatience)
I know the *bed*.

HE

I wake up there; I find you gone.

SHE

To the kitchen; for your tea, for my coffee.

HE

It's the same as every day.
                    (Tiny pause)
Is it *not?*

SHE

Yes; yes it is.

HE

This morning I wake in the king-size bed; I find you gone; I find you in the kitchen; I find nothing amiss.

SHE

No; nothing. I understand you.

HE

It's a day like every other day.

SHE

And I sympathize with you. I understand you, and I sympathize with you.

HE

We are each other's rod?

SHE *(Agreeing after a pause)*

So to speak.

HE

Nothing is amiss—except perhaps the coffee.

SHE *(Patient)*

Now, now.

(Afterthought)

You should taste the *tea.*

HE

It's a day like every other day—*except!*

SHE *(Vaguely embarrassed)*

Yes; I know.

HE

Except!

SHE

I said: I know.

HE

This afternoon you come to me and say you want the flowers for a vase *between* our *beds*.

SHE (*Sort of sad*)

Yes.

HE

Between . . . our *beds*.

SHE (*Glum and impatient*)

Yes; yes!

HE (*Overly calm*)

When did it happen?

SHE
(*Pretending not to comprehend*)

Hm?

HE

When did it happen? When did our lovely bed . . . split and become two? When did a table appear where there had been no space, in the center of our lovely bed?

SHE (*Very reasonable*)

Well, I suspect it's been coming.

HE

Pardon?

SHE
(*Closes her eyes momentarily*)
I suspect it's been coming.

HE
And those *beds!* They're not wide, those beds; they're single;
they're for a solitary, or for a corpse!

SHE
These things sneak up on you.

HE
Did you have someone in? Hm?
(SHE *shakes her head*)
Did the bed people come and take our lovely bed away and
leave these . . . these pallets? Hm?

SHE (*Apologetic*)
No one came: these things happen. We've been lucky.

HE (*Quietly authoritarian*)
I want an *answer* for this!
(SHE *sighs, smiles, shrugs*)
I want an ANSWER for this!!

SHE (*A trifle strident*)
Well, it happens sooner or later; look around you; look at our
friends. Sooner or later it happens. Maybe we'll be lucky and
it won't go any further.

HE (*After a second*)
Further? *Further!?*

SHE (*Quietly; shrugs*)
Of course: separate rooms.

HE (*Pause; quietly*)

Separate . . . oh, God.

(*Pause*)

BLACKOUT

ENTRE SCENE

As at the end of the previous scene.

HE (*As before*)

Oh God.

SHE (*Tentative*)

Yes; well.
(A *sign descends:* IDENTIFY YOURSELVES.
THEY *notice it simultaneously*)

HE

Oh. Of course; yes, of course. You want to go first?

SHE

No; you go.

HE (*Smiles*)

Please.

SHE (*Smiles*)

All right.
(SHE *stands. Improvisation:* SHE *tells a bit about
herself* [*the actress*], *her career—training, roles, etc.,*

then a bit about herself [kids, husband, etc.; fin
ishes with:])
There's more there in the program; you can read it—*after*
the play. I think the author would rather.
(To him)
Now you; you go.
(Sits)

H E
All right.
(Stands. Similar improvisation. Finishes with:)
Well, I think that's most of it.
(Sits.
The sign rises, disappears)

H E (As before)
Separate rooms . . . oh, God.
(SHE begins exiting)
Where are you going?

S H E
Off.
(SHE exits, leaving him sitting. Pause)

BLACKOUT

SCENE FIFTEEN

At the end of the previous entre scene.
HE alone on stage, except standing.

HE
(Clears his throat, speaks to the audience)
Which brings us, then, to a discussion of this thing called
. . . "premature grief."
(SHE rushes in)

SHE *(To HE)*
Not yet!
Not yet!
To the audience; friendly)
"Premature grief!" Well, yes; but not yet! I wish to discuss
protocol.
(HE rushes in)
(To HIM, privately)
Do you want to . . . you know, go off?

HE

Not yet!
Not yet!

SHE *(Slightly offended)*
I *beg* your pardon?

HE
The subject of *grief* may be premature—though I wonder—
but not prema*ture* grief; that is not premature; *that* is of an
urgency which . . .

SHE
Protocol! Protocol supersedes all things—grief, joy, all . . .
things. We would be nowhere without it. Everything *hangs*
on it.

HE *(Not friendly)*
On *protocol*.

SHE (*Chatty*)

Of course! There is nothing without *order;* we *know that* . . .
except chaos, I suppose, if anyone wants it.

HE (*Rather vague*)

I had a friend once, called his country place Chaos.

SHE (*On with the lecture*)

And well you no longer have him! All is order: mathematics,
freedom, cooking.

HE (*Turns to leave*)

I *will* go.

SHE (*Stops him*)

No! You stay and hear this!

HE

My bed is gone; I may not discuss grief . . .

SHE

It is; yes! And you will! All in time!

HE (*Rue*)

I don't *have* it.

SHE

Time? That's *all* you have. Who *said* it?

HE

Time? Too much and too little. I don't *know.*

SHE (*Vague*)

Someone.

HE (*Pause; snorts*)

Protocol!

SHE (*The teacher again*)

It is the coding of order: precedence, etiquette, formality.

HE

Fiddlesticks! It's a table of contents!

SHE (*Arguing*)

It *used* to be, back in the *Greek* days. Don't argue!

HE (*Moves to exit*)

I'm going.

SHE (*Superior smile*)

All tight-lipped and clenched and ready to start muttering?
Go *on*; go ahead.

HE (*Sort of a dare*)

Flip the coin of love and what do you find?

SHE (*Sighs, dismisses him*)

Hatred; yes; I know; we *all* know.

HE
(*Exiting; high-pitched imitating of her*)
"Protocol is the coding of order." Hunh!
(*Exits*)

SHE (*Pause; calm; to herself*)

Well, it *is*.
(*To the audience; very chatty*)
Look here! This is the problem! My sister and her husband
are giving a dinner party—to which we are invited, of course,

it being a close-knit family . . . closely knitted?—and she has presented me with a dilemma, not the *first* she has set in my lap, by a long shot, but the first in ages which I've found intellectually stimulating.

Two of the guests are dying—well, we all are, but these two are *closer* to it—and both are of equal importance, rank, one would have said at one time, both men and both fit to sit to my sister's right. The question is: which to put there.

The tricky part is this: One of the men knows he is dying; the other man does *not*—as far as can be gathered, or, *has* been gathered.

You would think—*one* would think, *might* think—the man who knows he is dying must be put to my sister's right, since everyone knows that he is dying, and he knows that everyone knows. The honor is both deserved and transparent. Protocol is served.

On the *other* hand, everyone also knows that the *other* man is dying, while we suspect that he does not, and isn't there, then, an honor due him based on the sympathy stemming from our special knowledge, plus the fact that he is of equal rank?

W*ere* he, however, to be placed to my sister's right, might he not, assuming he did not, after all, know already, *sense* the reason he had been placed there . . . in place of the other? *Might* he, conceivably, gain his first inkling of his approaching death or, perhaps as unfortunate, might he not reason that the other man had been misdiagnosed, was not dying at all, and propose a toast in celebration of the faulty diagnosis?

And think of the *other* man—the one who *knows* he is dying: might *he* not succumb to the theory of misdiagnosis him*self*, and go so far as to propose a toast in his own behalf? Or, more likely, might he not think we no longer care, and have dropped him in rank in our cruelty—in our haste to have him gone?

I have begged my sister to consider alternatives: cancel the party; disinvite both gentlemen; make it a *buffet!* This last being a stroke of near genius, I thought—and still *do!* But, no: it cannot be cancelled, for it is important to her husband, as are the two gentlemen, for a while, at any rate; and she does not like buffets—will not *have* one in her *house!*

I come to the conclusion that she is fond of the dilemma, which is not a kind conclusion, I grant; she, on the other hand, insists that protocol will give us the answer. And since protocol is—as she puts it—my "bag," it is for *me* to supply *her* with the solution.

I think what my sister has done—unintentionally, I will say, out of great sibling generosity—is: to fashion a test for protocol, so willful that protocol's function as the coding of order will be put into question. Civilization, in other words, will collapse.

That is an unsisterly thing to do, an unfriendly one, and it brings up once again all those old questions about veneer.

BLACKOUT

SCENE SIXTEEN

Same as the end of Scene 15; clearly a different scene, though.
HE *enters, comes a step or two in from an exitway.*

HE
(*Mildly curious tone; offhand*)
How many children do we have?

SHE (*Smiles; cheerful*)
Three.
(HE *just stands there. Her voice takes on a tiny edge*)
Three!
(HE *just stands there. Not believing it*)
Four?
(HE *just stands there. Reassuring herself*)
Three!
(HE *just stands there. Quite incredulous*)
Four!?
(SHE *exits.* HE *just stands there*)

BLACKOUT

SCENE SEVENTEEN

As at the end of Scene 16.

HE (*Standing; smiles*)
Which brings us, then, to a discussion of this thing called
. . . "premature grief."
(*Imitates her tone, but softer*)
"Not yet!
Not yet!"
(*His own voice again; nods*)
Yes; yet.
And premature to what? To the incident properly to be
grieved over, I believe. Properly? Incident? I grieve every day
—a little bit—over my *own* death; no time to, for *me*, when it
happens to me; and I grieve over *her* death, a little, every day,
assuming it may happen before mine. *I'll* have enough grief
left when—*if!*—the time comes.

Are those afraid of it who have so little? Afraid they might exhaust the supply—those old theories about semen, or "spunk" as we used to call it?

(*Flat, midwestern accent*)

"Ya only got a coupla thousand in ya; don't waste it in ya hand!"

(*His own voice again; scoffs*)

Premature grief? I don't believe it for a minute!

Auden used to say—you see? I come back to him—Auden is *reputed* to have said that he would imagine a lover's death, to see how it felt—for the sake of poetry, I wager.

(*Shrugs*)

Maybe he didn't deeply care; I imagine he did. It's good to get in touch with the mind now and again. No harm.

(*Begins to exit; reconsiders*)

Do you believe . . . do you believe the mind and the brain are separate entities? Some scientists are beginning to come back to that view. Scientists!

(*Pause*)

Really!

(*Exits*)

BLACKOUT

SCENE EIGHTEEN

Stage empty; SHE *enters.*

SHE

(*Nodding, smiling, relieved*)

Three!

(SHE *sees* HE *is not there; exits.* HE *enters*)

HE

Pardon?

(HE *sees* SHE *is not there; stays. Pause.*)

SHE *(Enters)*

Three!

HE
(Pause; no great enthusiasm; accepting a fact)
Aha!

(Pause; SHE *exits; blank expression)*

BLACKOUT

SCENE NINETEEN

As at the end of Scene 18, except HE *is sitting.*
SHE *enters, sucking a finger, a dishrag over one arm.*

SHE
(Quite businesslike, if a trifle preoccupied)
Walnuts.
Parsley.
Bone marrow.
Celery root.

(Suspicious)

Do you *love* me?

HE
(Pause; HE, *too, suspicious)*
Crème Brulée. What happened to the Crème Brulée?

SHE
(*Flat*)
There's no Crème Brulée.

HE
What do you mean there's no Crème Brulée?

SHE (*As before*)
There's no Crème Brulée.

HE (*Pause*)
There's *always* Crème Brulée.

SHE
Not today.
(*Pause; uncertain*)
Do you love me?

HE
(*Pause; shrugs; some distaste*)
Sure.
(*Pause; not too friendly*)
What happened?

SHE (*Sits; dispirited*)
You know that lovely caramel that coats the Crème Brulée.

HE
Yes! Yum-yum!

SHE
You *know* it. You know how it's *done:* the sugar, the maple sugar is sprinkled over the lovely custards—remember the lovely custards?

HE

Yes! Yum-yum!

SHE

And popped into the oven, so to caramelize.

HE

Yum-yum!

SHE

And then, at the end, into the broiler; under the broiler for a
little, so the sugar crusts—that lovely crust you love.

HE

Yes!

SHE

Under the broiler for just a moment, just enough. It is *not*
the time to straighten up, look out the window, unfocus your
eyes on some distant spot and daydream—ruminate; think.

HE

Certainly not!

SHE

For if you *do* that, your caramel will scorch, or worse: will
blacken, become hard, burned and *awful!*

HE

Ugh!

SHE

There is nothing for it then but to throw it all away . . .

HE

I should think so!

SHE

The pan as well.

HE (*Long pause; quiet tone*)

I see. Well. Indeed.

SHE (*Sighs heavily*)

So *that* is why . . .

HE (*A sad, soft truth*)

. . . there is no Crème Brulée.

SHE (*Suspicious*)

Do you love me?

HE (*Very grudging; coarse tone*)

Yeah.

SHE (*Apologetic*)

I can make you something else.

HE (*Rather cool*)

Yeah? What?

SHE (*Straining for forgiveness*)

What would you like?

HE (*Heavy*)

We got any pans left?

SHE (*Soft*)

Be nice.

HE

How about . . . how about that *other* thing you make . . .
that, uh . . . whatever you call it, Idiot's Delight?

SHE
(*Pause, 'til it comes to her*)
Raspberry *Fool!!* Oh! Yes; well, all right!

HE (*Brightening*)
I *like that.*

SHE (*Stands; brightens*)
Raspberry Fool it is!
(SHE *starts toward the exit, pauses; tentative again*)
Will you *love* me?

HE (*Looks up; big smile*)
You bet!

(*Exits*)

BLACKOUT

SCENE TWENTY

(SHE *enters;* HE *as before*)

SHE
There aren't any raspberries!

BLACKOUT

SCENE TWENTY-ONE

Both sitting; HE *reading; some silence.*

SHE (*Quite straightforward*)

If you *love* me . . . how do you *know* you love me?

HE (*Not looking up*)

"How do I love thee?
Let me count the ways?"

SHE

Be serious.

HE

I thought she *was*.

SHE

You be.

HE (*Looks up at her*)

I thought *I* was.

SHE

How *do* you know?

HE (*Speculates a little*)

Not enough I *do?*

SHE

Most of the time; not just now.

HE

What's with now?

SHE

(*Putting his question aside*)

I don't *know*. How *do* you know you *love* me?

HE

Right now? Seriously?

(*Indicates the audience*)

SHE (*No matter*)

Yes; right now; seriously.

HE

(*Tries to make light of it*)

You mean: some fella with a machete comes at us, breaks into the house, all mad-eyed and frothing, what would I do? Would I protect you or try to save *myself*? Something like *that*?

SHE

Don't be silly; what would anyone be doing with a *machete*? Be *reasonable*.

(*Pause; eyes narrowing a little*)

What *would* you do?

HE (*Quite open about it*)

Damned if *I* know! Protect you, probably—if the old animal instinct was working; give it a split-second of civilized thought, of course, and who's to say!?

(*More serious*)

I do *love* you, you know. I mean, I'm young enough to make a change if I wanted—start again, fully, without it being substitutive, or anything. I could *do* all that, but I'm not *going* to; I don't even *want* to.

SHE
(*Bitter and hopeful simultaneously*)
Do you cheat on me a lot?

HE (*Pause*)
No; I don't. Good phrasing.

SHE (*Noncommital*)
Hmmm.

HE
I *do* love you. Let well enough alone. If it's well enough . . .
let it alone.

SHE (*Noncommital*)
Hmmm.

HE (*Closing the subject*)
I *do* . . . *love* you.
(*Long pause; a half-amused afterthought*)
Do *you* love *me*?

SHE
(*Pause; very open, rather wistful*)
I don't *know*.
(*Pause; his mouth opens a little.* SHE *speaks as
gently as the subject will allow;* SHE *smiles to re-
assure him*)

SHE (*Continued*)
I *think* I do.
(*Pause. Slow fade*)

END

LISTENING

(*A Chamber Play*)

1975

LISTENING was commissioned as a radio play, but it has been composed so that it may be performed on a stage without change.

THE CHARACTERS

THE MAN   *Fifty, or so; a good head, good profile, longish grey hair, tall rather than short, body average to thin; dress, casual, but a bit flamboyant.*

THE WOMAN   *Fifty; plain, ample, tall, hair pulled back, little makeup, "sensible" clothes.*

THE GIRL   *Twenty-five, give or take; thin, fragile, pretty, dressed in a simple, lovely pastel.*

THE VOICE   *A recorded voice, not stagey.*

THE SET

A great, semi-circular wall. Maybe we see over the top of it— trees and sky behind, and maybe ivy hangs down, but the walls continue to the wings: a sort of cyclorama. Stone. In the center of the wall, coming out in a semicircle (reverse to that of the wall) as many feet in diameter as will make a graceful design for the size of the stage, a fountain pool, raised two or three steps. Above it, a monster head in half relief, the spigot of the fountain emerging from the mouth. A green stain down the wall from the spigot to the pool basin. Two benches, one to either side of the pool, following the shape of the wall. Hot, white light.

LISTENING was first performed on radio in 1976.

THE WOMAN	*Irene Worth*
THE MAN	*James Ray*
THE GIRL	*Maureen Anderman*

Co-Directed by

JOHN TYDEMAN *and* EDWARD ALBEE

LISTENING was first performed on stage at The Hartford Stage Co., January 28, 1977.

THE WOMAN	*Angela Lansbury*
THE MAN	*William Prince*
THE GIRL	*Maureen Anderman*

Directed by EDWARD ALBEE

THE MAN *sits on the edge of the fountain bowl; looks about; no haste; looks into the fountain bowl; looks off, back.*

THE VOICE

One.

THE MAN (*Nods to himself*)

Very much as promised. Great circular wall . . . *semi*-circular wall; granite, probably. Or is it marble? Well, *I* don't know. *And* the formal fountain here in the center; French fountain; Italianate. Italianate: those Florentine curves! Pool . . . empty. Ever filled? Well, yes, sometime, of course; back *then*. Back when all this . . . overgrowth was a formal garden—clipped and trained and planned and . . . *then* it was full, I imagine. *Were* you? Were you full? Back when all this was . . . back before it had all become . . . impersonal?

(*Pause. Nods*)

Very much as stated. The marble pool . . . *that* I'm sure of now; very . . . marble. And look at *you!* What a spigot you are! Monster head? Satyr? Which are you? Monstre,* probably . . . or God. Where does the water come from . . . came . . . where did the water come? From your mouth! Of course, right there! The green stain down your chin. What a fountain! Very much as announced.

(*Pause*)

---

* French pronunciation.

Very much as announced, indeed. All this was personal—long ago. Oh, turn of the century? Or brought over—stone by stone, numbered, lettered, *mis*numbered, *mis*lettered? No question of it: personal, once. Once. Once the walls were for the curious—to keep them *out*, when it was personal. And now they keep them *in*, do they not? The curious—the very curious, and the rest of us: the curious and the *less* curious. Once, someone who had all this would leave the structure— the Man . . . si . . . on—would leave the patio—God, what a sound it makes! You wouldn't think it would, outdoor and all, merely footfall; but what a sound, echoing out of doors like that!—would leave the patio, alone, or arm in arm, the sudden silence of the grass after all that echoing, pass through a bower and come on . . . all this, clipped, then, trained, planned . . . and at the end of it all . . . you: you monster, or God.

(Pause)

Very much as imagined . . . I would imagine. Would they come . . . *did* they come here, sit on the edge, trail a hand in, exchange empires? I fancy.

(Pause)

Very much as suggested, but . . .

(Talks to the air around him; vaguely accusatory)

All right, *I'm* here. Where are *you?* Where *are* you?

(Back as before)

Be here, she said; *I'll* show you something!

(Chuckles. Pause. More sober)

And many, I suppose, over all the years, many sentences like that. *Be* here! *I'll* show you something. Hands trailing, exchanging glances . . . empires, exchanging empires . . . or whatever.

(Sees someone off)

Ah! Finally!

(Calls)

Hel-*lo*-o!

THE VOICE

Two.

(*The* WOMAN *enters*)

THE MAN (*Rises; hearty*)

Be here, you said. *I'll* show you something.

THE WOMAN (*A big, deep laugh*)

Well, I *will*.

THE MAN (*Vaguely intimidated*)

You're *look*ing well.

THE WOMAN

I am? Well, it's a wonder.

(*Calls off*)

Hey! Come on, now!

(*Back*)

For my age, you mean?

THE MAN

(*Not entirely comfortable*)

Is *she* coming? Is *she* with you? No; for anything.

THE WOMAN (*Stretches*)

Well . . . I may have a few pounds now where ounces were, and . . . what did Houseman say . . . "A dewlap nestles in the chinfolds, now, where once . . . ?" Or something. *And* . . . once you're fifty . . .

THE MAN

Not a chance!

THE WOMAN (*Chuckles*)

Oh, go sit down!

(HE *does*; SHE *calls off*)

THE WOMAN (*Continued*)
Come on! Don't dawdle; you'll forget where you are!

THE MAN
I thought *I* was the only one past *that* mark.

THE WOMAN
Forgetting where you were, or fifty? It comes on little poet's feet, and clubs you in the back of the head. You've stayed thin . . . thinnish; not much, but thinnish. And that orator's profile; that Emperor! I *like* that.

THE MAN (*An actor's reading*)
Hold my hand!

THE WOMAN (*Laughs*)
Don't be silly.
(*Calls off*)
Come on, you!

THE MAN (*Considers it*)
Don't hold my hand.

THE WOMAN (*Calls off*)
Don't dawdle!

THE MAN
(*To himself, but so* SHE *will hear*)
You *did* hold my hand.

THE WOMAN (*Stretches*)
I've held everybody's hand.
(*Pause; a twinkle*)
And, *did* I? *Did* I hold your hand?
(*Looks off again*)

THE MAN
(*Pause; rational consideration*)
Did you hold my hand?
(*Conversational*)
Is she coming?

THE WOMAN
(*Rises; sighs*)
Oh, I'd better see. She may have tripped on a leaf, or become
a butterfly. We're a fairy today, don't you know.

THE MAN
We *are!*

THE WOMAN (*None too pleased*)
Yes; we are.
(*Moving off*)
Don't dawdle, I said; where are you now, hunh?
(SHE *exits whence* SHE *entered*)

THE VOICE
Three.

THE MAN
(*To himself; very reasonable, dispassionate, inter-
ested; a proposition*)
Did we hold hands.
(*Pause; another*)
Did I hold your hand.
(*Pause; another*)
Did you hold my hand.
(*Pause; conclusion*)
We held hands.

THE VOICE

Four.

(*The* WOMAN *reenters, one hand around the* GIRL'*s arm; businesslike*)

THE WOMAN

Here we are; I've got her.

THE MAN (*Slightly sad*)

Such a pretty little thing.

THE WOMAN

We weren't a fairy at all; nor had we become a butterfly.

THE MAN (*"Really"*)

No!

THE WOMAN

No; we were a statue, or a forest thing, one or the other—near a tree, fronds and dapple; very still; quite invisible if you pretended not to see.

(*The* GIRL *wrenches her arm away, sits on the steps of the pool. The* MAN *moves to one side; the* WOMAN *sits on one of the benches*)

THE MAN (*As before*)

Pretty thing.

THE WOMAN (*Arranging her skirt*)

Oh? You like that . . . tightness around the mouth, that . . . assumptive air? Matriarch at twenty-two, or whatever?

THE MAN (*Determined*)

Well, she looks pretty there by the fountain—sad; pretty.
(*Smiles*)
A resting butterfly, if I may.

THE WOMAN (*Scoffs*)

A butterfly! More like a . . . a praying mantis. *That's* it! A praying mantis; I've been looking for it! Watch her; she won't move now; she'll stay where she is, listening, planning, judging . . .

THE MAN

Judging?

THE WOMAN

. . . when it's safe—to move; to jump? She'll wait it out. *Us* out. She'll try to wait it out.

THE MAN
(*A little remote; a joke, nonetheless*)
Did she devour her husband? They do, you know—the mantis, the female. Has she had one?

THE WOMAN (*Her big laugh again*)

No! Her!? No!

THE MAN
She looks so . . . Shall I talk to her? Shall I go over?

THE WOMAN (*Snorts; laughs*)

You go right ahead.

THE MAN
And that means . . . ?

THE WOMAN
That means you go right ahead. I always say what I mean.

THE MAN
(*A statement; a question*)
She won't bite me.

THE WOMAN

Let you get close, your guard down, and then—crack!—right in the neck? Like that?

THE MAN

Something like that.

THE WOMAN (*Wrinkles her nose*)

Nothing like that.

THE MAN (*Dubious*)

Well . . .

THE WOMAN

Nothing *like* that! I *told* you! It's not actually the neck, is it.

THE MAN

No.

THE WOMAN

No; they chew the head right off, don't they—the mantis? During the act, as they say?

THE MAN (*Sad*)

As they say. Look at her!

THE WOMAN
(*Turns her gaze languidly*)

Mmmmmmmm.

THE MAN

Why is she doing that? With her mouth?

THE WOMAN
(*As the* GIRL *opens and shuts her mouth, a bit like a frog; calm and preoccupied*)

Open and close; open and close. That it?

THE MAN

Is she . . . what? Gulping for air?

THE WOMAN (*Doctrinaire*)

No; she's opening and closing her mouth. Is that simple enough? She's breathing perfectly well; let her alone: she'll stop.

THE MAN

Well, hyperventilation is known to be . . .

THE WOMAN
(*Through her teeth; curiously angry*)
She is not hyperventilating! I hate that term!

THE MAN (*Retreating; defensive*)

Oh. Well. If you say.

THE WOMAN (*That laugh*)
She's . . . well, I *know* her; I know what she does.
(*Smiles*)
Go talk to her.

THE MAN

Hm?

THE WOMAN

Go *talk* to her. Sidle on over; sit down next to her—well, near; not on top, or she might bolt—mantis or no.

THE MAN (*Accusatory*)
Why don't *you* talk to her?

THE WOMAN
I've *talked* to her. *You* talk to her.

THE WOMAN
(*Pleased with her idea*)
Tell her something interesting; tell her something she can chew on.

(*Laughs*)
Tell her you do her food.

THE MAN (*Shy*)
Oh . . .

THE WOMAN (*Full of enthusiasm*)
Tell her! Tell her you do her food! God, she eats enough! What does she do with it?She must throw it up! Go tell her!

THE MAN
(*Rises; moves toward the* GIRL)
All right.

THE WOMAN
Gently, though; don't be abrupt.

THE MAN (*Approaching*)
She knows I'm coming; she senses it.

THE WOMAN
That's all right.

THE MAN
(*Admiration; tenderness*)
She *is* an animal, isn't she.

THE WOMAN (*Laughs*)
Oh *ho*; you've found it out. That's close enough; she knows you're there. Say it. Say whatever you're going to. Softly.

THE MAN (*Softly; gently*)

Hello; I do your food.

(*Pause*)

THE VOICE

Five.

THE WOMAN (*Giggles*)

Say it again! I love it!

THE MAN

Shall I?

THE WOMAN

Oh, yes! Please! Please!

THE MAN (*Gently*)

Hello; I do your food.
                    (*The* WOMAN *giggles again*)
Nothing. Will she . . . can she . . . just not listen?

THE WOMAN

She listens. She may even speak to *you*.

THE MAN

I'll say it again. Shall I?

THE WOMAN (*Eyes closed; giggles*)

Good.

THE MAN (*Leans forward*)

Hello; I do your food.
                    (*The* WOMAN *giggles softly*)
She's turning toward me.
                    (*Gasps*)
Oh! The eyes! Such beautiful, beautiful eyes!

THE WOMAN

Mmmmmmmm.

THE MAN (*To the* GIRL; *a whisper*)

I do your food.

THE WOMAN
(*Eyes closed until notice*)

Anything?

THE MAN (*Still gentle*)

I say: I do your food.

THE WOMAN

Something?

THE MAN
(*Shoots a silencing hand out*)

SHHHH!

THE WOMAN

Oh? Is she going to?

THE MAN
(*To the* GIRL; *leaning in; urgent*)

Yes? Go on. Speak

THE GIRL (*A little "away"*)

You do . . . what?

THE MAN (*Patient*)

I do your food.

THE GIRL (*Face all screwed up*)

What?!

THE MAN
(*Mortified, but persisting*)

I . . . I do your food.

THE WOMAN ("*I told you so*")

You wanted to *talk* to her.

THE MAN (*Offended*)

Hush, you!
(*To the* GIRL; *a little too slow, too precise*)

I—do—your—food.

THE GIRL
(*Nods slowly, knowingly; speaks softly*)

I do *your* food.
(*The* WOMAN *laughs quietly*)

THE MAN
(*Wheedling; disapproving*)

Oh . . . hush, I said.
(*To the* GIRL)

No; no, you don't.

THE GIRL (*Absolutely flat*)

I don't do your *food*.
(*The* WOMAN *laughs quietly*)

You do my . . . what?

THE MAN

Food.

THE GIRL
(*Considers; shakes her head*)

No.
(*The* WOMAN *laughs quietly*)

THE VOICE

Six.

THE WOMAN

Oh, that was splendid!

THE MAN (*Serious reproach*)

You don't *help.*

THE WOMAN (*Quietly pleased*)

Well . . . I didn't intend to.

THE MAN
(*Sees the* GIRL *has withdrawn into herself*)

She's gone back *into* herself.

THE WOMAN
(*Looks over at the* GIRL *who is staring into the pool
again*)

Do it again: say your sentence.

THE MAN (*Will not be mortified*)

No-o!

THE WOMAN

Oh . . . *do!*

THE MAN

No; stop it; no.

THE WOMAN

You have no adventure.
(*Mocking tone*)

"You lack adventure."

THE MAN (*Rebuke*)

Oh!

THE WOMAN
(*Pleased with a secret*)

You want her to *talk?*

THE MAN

Well, she *did.*

THE WOMAN

More, I mean. A whole . . . you want to hear a *lot?*

THE MAN (*Embarrassed*)

I don't care.

THE WOMAN

Are you embarrassed?
(*Laughs*)

Are you embarrassed?

THE MAN (*Too loud*)

Yes! Have her talk!
(*Under his breath*)

I don't care *what* you do.

THE WOMAN

Oh yes you do!

THE MAN (*Tight-lipped*)

All right; I *care* what you do.

THE WOMAN (*A smug smile*)

You bet you do!

THE MAN
(*Shakes his head, devout in denial*)

No!

THE WOMAN

Watch me, now!
(*Raises both arms for attention*)
I said: watch me!

THE MAN
(*Looking away, at the* GIRL)

I am.

THE WOMAN

Not her! Who do you think I *am?* Me! Watch me!

THE MAN
(*Weary; turns and looks at the* WOMAN)
All right; I'm watching.

THE WOMAN
(*Rather like a magician*)
I will snap my fingers . . . and *she* will snap; she will snap
to, or, "it up." *She* . . . will snap.

THE MAN (*Annoyed and puzzled*)

What!?

THE WOMAN

W*atch* me!

THE MAN

All right!

THE WOMAN

Watch *me*, and then watch *her!* Watch *me!*
(SHE *snaps her fingers, looking at the* GIRL)
And now . . . look *there*.

THE VOICE

Seven.
(*The* GIRL *reacts to the finger-snap rather like a
timid animal;* SHE *tenses, senses her surroundings,
then "humanizes" again, prepares for a conversation,
considers something in the pool, laughs, none too
cheerfully*)

THE GIRL

You don't *listen*.

THE WOMAN
(*As if the* MAN *were not there*)
Well, that may *be*.

THE GIRL

Pay attention, rather, is what you don't do. Listen: oh, yes;
carefully, to . . . oh, the sound an idea makes . . .

THE WOMAN

. . . a *thought*.

THE GIRL

No; an idea.

THE WOMAN

As it does what?

THE GIRL

(*Thinks about that for a split second*)

Mmmmmmmm . . . as the chemical thing happens, and then the electric thing, and then the muscle; *that* progression. The response—that almost reflex thing, the movement, when an idea happens.

(A *strange little smile*)

That *is* the way the brain works, is it not? The way it functions? Chemical, then electric, then muscle?

(*The woman does an "et voilà!" gesture*)

THE MAN (*Quiet awe*)

Where does it come from?

THE WOMAN

What?

THE MAN

The . . . all that. Where does it come from?

THE WOMAN

I haven't found out. It all begins right there: she says, "You don't listen." Every time, she says: "You don't listen."

THE MAN

To what!? You don't listen to what!?

THE WOMAN (*Sotto voce*)

I don't *know* what I don't listen to.

THE MAN (*Accusatory*)

Yes, and do you care?

THE WOMAN (*So reasonable*)

I don't *know*.

THE MAN (*Snorting*)

Of course not!

THE WOMAN (*Quite brusque*)

Defend the overdog once in a while, will you!? At least what you *think* it is. How do you know who's what!?

THE MAN

I don't!

THE WOMAN

All right!

THE MAN
(*Shrugs; throws it away*)

Get behind that sentence, that's all you have to do. Find out what precedes.
(*Shrugs again*)

THE WOMAN
(*Nods; smiles ruefully*)

Thanks.

THE GIRL

Me! We're talking to me!

THE WOMAN (*To herself*)

I do pay attention. And I hear. I'm ready for a lot.

THE GIRL (*A dare*)

Are you? You!

THE WOMAN
(*To the* GIRL)

Am I what?

THE GIRL

Do you pay attention? *Do* you hear? *Are* you ready for a lot?

THE WOMAN (*Puzzles; recalls*)

Oh! *I* see. Well . . . I'd *know.*

THE GIRL

What! If I were . . . to do what?

THE WOMAN (*Languidly*)

Oh . . . say there was glass in there, in the fountain there—sharp glass.

(*Pause; interest*)

Is there?

THE GIRL (*Looks*)

No; and no water, either—all dry. Leaves, a strand of . . . ivy, all dry; dead ivy; a stone, and the basin is all set with pebbles; it's rough between them; smooth pebbles. No sharp glass.

THE WOMAN

If there were, I'd know. Rather, I'd know if you saw it.

THE GIRL

That it was sharp glass?

THE WOMAN

No: that I should pay attention.

THE GIRL

I'm full of guile.

THE WOMAN

But I'd *know.*

THE GIRL

There are so *many* things I could do.

THE WOMAN

Yes? What?

THE GIRL

Say—for example—see how the marble has a waterline, and
you'd never look; that's *one* way. Whine, and say I'm hot
and don't want the sun anymore; scratch my leg.

THE WOMAN
(*Claps her hands softly*)

Very *good*.

THE GIRL

Nothing unsubtle; nothing like reach and pull back, or hold
my breath, or . . . start chattering—running on, as they say.
Oh, I'd be subtle.

THE WOMAN

Of course; but I'd *know*.

THE GIRL

What!

THE WOMAN (*Calm*)

That you'd found glass . . . sharp glass.

THE GIRL

You *say* you would.

THE WOMAN

I told you: I pay attention. They all make sounds—your
chemical thing and your electric thing. I can . . . I can hear
your pupils widen.

THE GIRL (*Smiles*)

No you can't.

THE WOMAN

Sharp senses. And the decision *not* to hold the breath . . . that breaks a pattern, too.

THE GIRL (*Breaks in*)

I used to take sharp glass, when I was little and sunburned —brown, not burned—sunbrown, and scrape it along my leg, pretend it was a scalpel; take off the top scale; just that, leave an irregular white path, thin as a thread. The skin below my knees was . . . so glistening. In the summer.

THE WOMAN

Where would you find it?

THE GIRL

Hm?

THE WOMAN

You would *find* it.

THE GIRL

The sharp glass?

THE WOMAN

Mmmmmmmm.

THE GIRL (*Laughs*)

Oh . . . sitting somewhere, seeing the waterline on the marble, or a bottle on the beach, the bottom showing. Pick it up and always broken off just at the bottom. There's lots of sharp glass when you're little. Always. And . . . there's enough later.

THE WOMAN

You're *sure* there's none *there* . . . in the fountain.

THE GIRL
(*Looks back into the fountain*)
No. The skeleton of a mouse; half a blue egg; a feather.

THE WOMAN (*Pressing a little*)

And no glass.

THE GIRL

No.

(*Pause*)

Who built it?

THE WOMAN

What?

THE GIRL (*Impatient*)
Egg! Feather! Mouse! All this!

THE WOMAN (*Shrugs*)
Well, *I* don't know.

THE GIRL (*Puzzled*)

Don't you?

(*Pause; some pique*)

Yes you do!

THE WOMAN

I do?

THE GIRL (*Enraged*)

Yes! You do!

THE WOMAN (*Venomous*)

Subside!

(SHE *clicks her fingers*)

Subside.

(*The* GIRL *subsides*)

THE VOICE

Eight.

THE MAN

Subside?

THE WOMAN

Sure. *It* works: look at her.

THE MAN

Stop and start.

THE WOMAN

And caution.

(*Laughs*)

Oh, don't look at me with those eyes; one of you's enough
. . . the "intensity."

THE MAN

How long have I known you?

THE WOMAN

(*Cheerful; even coquettish*)

I don't know. Ever? Who knows a lady? Spaniel eyes; does
'ums have a problem?

THE MAN

(*Dismisses her with a gesture*)

I don't know. Go back to *her*.

THE WOMAN

All right. Watch me, now!
(SHE *snaps her fingers*)

THE VOICE

Nine.

THE GIRL
(*Everything as before*)

You don't listen!

THE WOMAN (*Soft laugh*)

Well, that may be.

THE GIRL

Pay attention, rather, is what you don't do. Half a blue egg?
Half a blue *egg?* I didn't say shell; I said egg.

THE WOMAN

Yes, I know, but it wasn't there . . . nor the mouse bones,
nor the feather, so . . . it could be what you said, easily
enough. *And* . . . I *thought* you meant shell: half a blue
shell. But it doesn't matter, does it?

THE GIRL

Do they ever . . . is it ever filled up?

THE WOMAN

In rain.

THE GIRL

Not . . . not just filled?

THE WOMAN (*Two replies*)

No. I don't think so.

THE GIRL

Never?

THE WOMAN (*Getting peevish*)

Not *now!*

THE GIRL
(*Gazing at the fountainhead*)

Turned on? Neptune there?

THE MAN

Neptune! Of course!

THE WOMAN (*Unconvinced*)

Who?

THE GIRL

Neptune: Roman version of the Egyptian Hapyi, the Greek
Poseidon. Isn't that who it is there? "Fountainhead?" Water
dribbling off his chin, then coming down like a little boy,
on the pebbles, peeing, then like in a tunnel—that hollow
sound when there's water there? Don't they . . . don't you
. . . isn't it ever filled?

THE WOMAN

I said: no.

THE GIRL

Reason?

THE WOMAN
(*Daring contradiction*)

I don't know.

THE GIRL

I wish they . . . I wish it would.

THE WOMAN (*Pause; smile*)

Certainly.

(*Pause*)

What! Are you stopping? Nothing more to say?

THE GIRL

(*Looking back down into the pool*)

Well, you say the mouse is not there—the shell of *it*, the skeleton; the feather; the blue shell. It takes some thinking about . . . if they're not there.

THE WOMAN

Why? Do *you* see them?

THE GIRL

I said: it takes some thinking about. I didn't *say* I saw them.

(*A smile; daring the* WOMAN)

Nor that I did.

(SHE *looks back into the pool*)

THE WOMAN

(*Turning away; slightly contemptuous*)

Look away, Dixie*land*.

THE VOICE

Ten.

THE MAN

How do they say? "You're small of spirit."

THE WOMAN (*Unperturbed*)

Which one of us? Who?

THE MAN (*Apologetically*)

You, of course.

THE WOMAN (*Expansive*)

Why not her!?

THE MAN

I don't . . . *know* her.

THE WOMAN (*Mimicking*)

You don't . . . *know* me.

THE MAN

I *thought* so.

THE WOMAN (*Hoots*)

By what right? Holding a hand, or not? Holding whatever . . . or not? What did you hold? What did you *not* hold? Hunh?

THE MAN (*Weary*)

Never mind; leave off.

THE WOMAN

"Let me hold it! Please! Oh, God, I want to hold it!" And then they can't remember—eventually . . . A, if they did, and, B, if they did, what it was.

THE MAN (*Contemptuous*)

Or was not.

THE WOMAN

Go back to your pots.

THE MAN
(*Reasonable, if rather pleased with the information*)

You're just . . . not nice.

THE WOMAN (*Shrugs*)

Who's nice?

THE MAN

Lots of people.
(*Points to the* GIRL)
She is, probably.

THE WOMAN

Oh? Shall I show you? You want another example?

THE MAN (*Weary*)

Sure.
(*Sad chuckle*)
Are you going to disillusion me?

THE WOMAN

Oh, not deep down.
(*Raises her hand*)
Watch me, now.
(*Snaps her fingers*)

THE VOICE

Eleven.

THE GIRL
(*Snaps to; overly enthusiastic*)
You don't listen!

THE WOMAN

Well, that may be.

THE GIRL (*Correcting herself*)
Pay attention, rather, is what you don't do.

THE WOMAN

Now, about the girl yesterday . . .

THE GIRL (*Right in*)

What girl yesterday? She deserved it!

THE WOMAN (*To the* MAN)

Pay attention, you!

THE MAN

I'm here.

THE WOMAN (*To the* GIRL)

She deserved it?

THE GIRL

She deserved it!

THE WOMAN

But so *hard*. And why did you make a fist? Why not your open hand?

THE GIRL

I would have hurt it. Besides: she stole.

THE WOMAN
(*A quiet, even correction*)

Borrowed; she borrowed.

THE GIRL

Stole!

THE WOMAN (*Reasonable*)

No one would steal what she borrowed.

THE GIRL

Things are borrowed just because they're returned? Stolen things are returned, too.

THE WOMAN

Seldom willfully.

THE GIRL
(*Sulking; tension underneath* **it**)
My cardboard was returned? Willfully?

THE WOMAN

Yes!

THE MAN

Her what?

THE WOMAN (*Impatient*)
Her cardboard.

THE GIRL
My cardboard? You say she returned it!

THE WOMAN (**Abrupt**)
Yes! Returned! Willfully!

THE GIRL

After I *hit* her.

THE WOMAN

She hadn't had it long. It wasn't even off the table; her hand was just on it—feeling it, stroking it, not grasping. You made a decision.

THE GIRL

I did not!

THE WOMAN

That she had stolen.

THE GIRL

So did you! That she had borrowed.

THE WOMAN

She said, "Let me look at it." That's all she said to you, isn't
it? Wasn't it? Did she say anything more? Did she indicate
anything?

THE GIRL

Guile.

THE WOMAN

Indeed!

THE GIRL

Guile.

THE WOMAN (*Chiding*)

Not everything. Not . . . every*one*; not everything.

THE GIRL

She!

THE WOMAN

She, too, hunh?

THE GIRL

Hm?

THE WOMAN
"Such pretty cardboard," she said; "such pretty blue cardboard." And she touched it; just that; and you hit her . . .
with a fist, not even open hand . . .
                 (*Afterthought*)
ded; openhanded.

THE GIRL
     (*A general statement; an announcement*)
There are things and things. Things to which rules apply—
"the" rules—and things to which . . . to which they do not.
And that is that.
             (*To the* MAN)
You! There are things and things, aren't there!?

THE MAN (*Startled*)
Me!

THE WOMAN (*Amused; vitalized*)
You! She's talking to you! It's your chance; don't botch it!

THE MAN
But . . .

THE GIRL (*To the* MAN; *again*)
There are things . . . and things. Did you *hear* me? Are *you*
real?

THE WOMAN (*Head back; relaxing*)
Just listen; be nice; nod; smile once or twice; encourage her.
        (*The* MAN *leans toward the* GIRL)
That's it; lean in.

THE MAN (*To the* GIRL; *private*)
There are things and things; yes.

THE GIRL

(*Giggles a little; sharing a confidence*)

Yes. Most cardboard is grey . . . or brown, heavier. But blue is . . . unusual. That would be enough, but if you see blue cardboard, tile blue, love it, want . . . it, and have it . . . then it's special. But—don't interrupt me!

THE WOMAN (*Startled*)

I'm not!

THE MAN

Don't interrupt her!

THE WOMAN (*Annoyed*)

I'm not!

THE GIRL (*Exaggerated woe*)

Neither of you cares.

THE MAN

I *care*.

THE WOMAN

He cares!

(*Afterthought*)

And you *know* about *me*.

THE GIRL (*Snorts*)

You!

(*Back to the* MAN)

Well, if you want more value from it, from the experience, and take *grey* cardboard, mix your colors and paint it, carefully, blue, to the edges, smooth, then it's not *any* blue cardboard but very special: grey cardboard taken and made blue, self-made, self-made blue—better than grey, better than the other blue, because it's self-done. Very valuable, and even looking at it is a theft; touching it, even to take it to a window to see the smooth lovely color, all blue, is a theft. Even the knowledge of it is a theft . . . of sorts.

THE WOMAN
(*To the* MAN; *smiling unpleasantly*)
So, take care!

THE GIRL
Ignore her. Very special.

THE WOMAN
(*Leans toward the* GIRL)
But had you *done* that?

THE GIRL (*Sharp*)
What!?

THE MAN (*Puzzled*)
What!?

THE GIRL (*Sharper*)
What!?

THE WOMAN (*Patient smile*)
Taken the grey and carefully made it blue?

THE GIRL
(*Imitates the* WOMAN's *tone and smile*)
It was what I would do it from. It was the model; it was the blue from which I would have made my own. It was the model.

THE WOMAN
So you *didn't* . . . *do* all that.

THE GIRL

It was the model! I would have done it *from* it!

THE WOMAN

Not even *worth* taking.

THE GIRL

It was the *model!* It was worth *taking!*

THE WOMAN

Half, then—half what you said it was; half worth taking. Mitigation; always mitigation.

THE GIRL (*Chin raised*)

Half a theft is worse than none.
                    (*Smiles; quite pleased*)

THE WOMAN (*At no one*)

She's a sad girl.
                    (*Sees the* MAN *is about to react*)
No, no; not this one; the other one; the one she struck at.

THE MAN (*Sad irony*)

Ah. Not this one.

THE WOMAN (*To the* GIRL)

She's a sad girl. You! She's a sad girl!

THE GIRL
(*Not really interested*)

Yes? She is?

THE WOMAN (*A catalogue*)

Parents dead; baby dead; husband to the wild wind; catatonic sometimes; others . . . well, not pretty. You caught her at a *good* time. You're not the only one with a couple of problems. Learn to look around you.

THE GIRL
(*Laughs abruptly; leans toward the fountain*)
Well, if I were to do *that* . . . I might find something useful—hyperbolic, but . . . useful.

THE WOMAN
I didn't mean to look around. By look around, I didn't mean to look around. I meant . . . look *around.*
(*Pause*)
Is there anything there? In the fountain? Anything new?

THE GIRL
There's nothing—except what I said, and who knows about that? Look around me?
(*Sad*)
There's nothing. What did the nice one say? You have a past; look for it.
(*Looks into the fountain; shakes her head*)
Well, I'm looking. There's nothing.

THE WOMAN (*Gently*)
Well, you have the blue in a piece of cardboard.
(*Sees a refusal to react*)
No? Closing up again? All right.

THE MAN (*Quietly*)
Let her alone.

THE WOMAN (*Sarcastic*)
You see a tear? Is the lower lip a-tremble? The dimple puckered?

THE MAN (*Sad smile*)

No. Just . . . just nothing. Forget it.

THE WOMAN (*Patronizing*)

All right.

(*To the* GIRL; *brusque*)

You! You in the dress! Did I tell you she cried?

(*The* GIRL *shakes her head; pauses, shakes it again, longer*)

No? Well . . . yes. You hit her and she cried; cause and effect.

THE GIRL (*Shakes her head*)

No she didn't; I didn't see it, so it didn't happen: cause and effect.

THE WOMAN

(*Grudging admiration*)

You *are* a *wonder!* Well, she did; she did cry. Does that make you feel anything?

THE GIRL

(*As if discovering it for the first time*)

Why is there no *water?*

THE WOMAN

And so much for *that,* hunh? Choose a subject out of the hat? Play pickatopic? Well, we'll come *back* to it, you can't go 'round striking people . . .

THE GIRL (*Strident*)

Why is there no *water!*

THE MAN (*After a pause*)

Tell her.

THE WOMAN

No; *I'll* pick a subject.

THE MAN (*Pleading a little*)

Tell her.

THE WOMAN

You tell her. Subject: *I* used to come here.

THE GIRL (*Hisses it*)

You never did!

THE WOMAN

He . . . and I did.
   (*The* MAN *straightens up, startled*)

THE GIRL (*Quite offended*)

No!

THE MAN (*Correcting*)

No now, you and I, we never . . .

THE WOMAN (*Curt; contemptuous*)

I said *he; he!* Are you *he?* I said *he* and I. What are you
assuming? Both of you!

THE MAN

Well, I mean . . . anyone.

THE WOMAN

No; not anyone; I'm not your come into the garden, Maude;
nor am I Maude; but ooooohhhhh . . . yessssss, *I* used to
come here.

THE GIRL

It was him! That one there! Wasn't it!

THE MAN

No; no; *listen.*

THE GIRL

WHO THEN!?

THE WOMAN (*Offhand; teasing*)

Oh . . . one of my beaux.

THE GIRL

Well . . . never mind about it! The cardboard! The blue!
I'm talking about *that!*

THE WOMAN (*Dreamy*)

Yes; I know.

THE GIRL (*Dogmatic*)

Blue. That is the subject.

THE WOMAN (*Ibid*)

Yes; I know.

THE WOMAN (*Recalling*)

We would come here, and I would begin to understand
things, I think, or . . . appreciate them, certainly . . . *like*
them, at any rate.

THE WOMAN

Quite together, he not much older; but in *those* days . . .

THE WOMAN

. . . one was much younger than one *was.*
(*Sees the* GIRL *reaching for something*)
DON'T DO THAT!! GET YOUR HAND OUT OF THE
POOL!
(*The* GIRL *stops; it has been nothing*)

THE WOMAN (*Continued*)

I'm *not* a stupid woman . . . nor a slow one. Or, have you gathered?

(*Pause*)

THE MAN (*To fill the silence*)

You asking me?

THE WOMAN (*Smiles*)

No. Her. I'm not a stupid woman . . . or have you gathered?

THE GIRL (*Glum*)

You do all right.

THE WOMAN (*Pleased*)

I thought I did.

THE GIRL (*Grudging*)

Well enough.

THE WOMAN

Thank you. *Is* there something there all of a sudden, by the way? In the pool? Or were you testing me, moving like that?

THE GIRL (*Defiant; quiet*)

Who are *you?*

THE WOMAN
(*Amused; pretends confusion*)

Who *am* I?

THE MAN
(*Not really expecting an answer*)

How many? And when? And was it?

THE WOMAN
(*Answering him, in a way*)

Who am *I*?

THE GIRL

You *did* know, then.

THE WOMAN

What? What did I know then?

THE GIRL (*Mumbles*)

Whether it was filled up—a long time ago; whether it was filled up.

THE WOMAN

Speak up!

THE GIRL

Whether it was filled up! If it was filled up!

THE WOMAN
(*Pretending not to have heard*)

When!?

THE GIRL

You were here! When you were here!

THE WOMAN
(*Thinks about it for a moment*)

Well, I wouldn't necessarily have known, would I? I *did* . . . but I needn't have. How long ago *was* it?

THE GIRL
(*Tentative; after a pause*)

How long ago was it?

THE WOMAN (*Eyes closed*)

Hmmmmmmmm?

THE GIRL (*Pleading*)

How long?

THE WOMAN
(A *slow smile; spreads it out*)

A long time ago.

THE VOICE

Twelve.

THE MAN
(*As the* WOMAN *hmmmmmmms and chuckles—closemouthed—throughout*)

Did you?
(*Pause*)
Did you know?
(*Pause*)
Did you come here with someone else, and did you know?
(*Pause*)
W*as* it full?
(*Pause*)
Was it *full?*
(*Pause*)
Did you come here with someone else?
(*Pause*)
Did you know?
(*Pause*)
Did you?
(*Pause*)

THE VOICE

Thirteen.

THE WOMAN (*Laughs*)

Nosey, aren't you.

THE MAN (*Shrugs*)

It's reasonable.

THE WOMAN (*Sighs*)

Nothing is reasonable.
(*Raises a hand*)
Watch me, now; snap the fingers.
(SHE *does; The* GIRL *comes to attention as before*)

THE GIRL
(*High-handed accusation*)

You don't *listen*.

THE WOMAN
(*Soft laugh; a look at the* MAN)

Well, that may be.

THE GIRL

Pay attention, rather, is what you don't do. Cry? She cried!?
The girl: she cried?

THE WOMAN (*After a moment*)

Oh, yes.

THE GIRL

Over sky blue!

THE MAN

Sky blue?

THE WOMAN

Cardboard. Can't you retain?

THE MAN (*Offended*)

Well, mostly; not . . . *some* things; the perverse, the obscure, the out of kilter. *I* can follow pretty well, most things.

THE GIRL (A *dare*)

Over sky blue!?

THE WOMAN

Over sky blue?

(*Laughs gently*)

Oh, my, yes; one of the most frequent. Sky blue? Very frequently; more even than rain—sadness in the face of beauty, day following night—relief: tears of relief; oh, my; or for no reason at all . . . merely how blue it is. Speech after long silence? Remember?

(*Pause*)

No?

(*Pause; the* GIRL *shakes her head stubbornly*)

Nothing subtle for you, hunh! Just the *hard* stuff to get *you* crying, eh?: blood?, or shadows on the wall?, or footsteps?

THE GIRL

(*Very loud; clearly a new subject*)

When did you come here?

THE WOMAN

Oh, you're up to that again.

THE GIRL

When did you *come* here?

THE WOMAN

Hmmmmmm?

THE GIRL

When!

THE MAN (*Quiet pleading*)

Tell her; please.

THE GIRL (*Close to hysteria*)

When!? When did you *come* here!?

THE WOMAN
(*Too loud, too slow, too distinct*)

A—very—long—time—ago.
(*Then, an afterthought*)
The benches were only *this high*.
(SHE *gestures and laughs*)

THE GIRL (*Puzzles; laughs*)

Silly!

THE WOMAN

What if *she* had hit *you? Back*, I mean?

THE GIRL
(*Thinks a moment; chuckles*)
Well, and I would have hit *her* back.
(*Louder, and triumphant*)
That would have brought them running!
(*A loud laugh*)

THE WOMAN

Yes, but what if it hadn't?
(*The* GIRL *doesn't respond; stares into the pool*)
Don't look down all the time.
(*Pause; no response*)
All right; *look* down all the time.

THE VOICE

Fourteen.

THE MAN (*Reaffirming*)

You're *not* nice.

THE WOMAN
(*Smiles; mimics her reply from before*)

Who's *nice?*

THE MAN (*Rather vacant*)

Oh . . . *some* people are.

THE WOMAN

Well, *that* may be.

THE MAN (*Laughs brusquely*)

Ha! Don't start in with *me!* That phrase won't work with *me.*
Don't try to snap *me* to attention; I won't *follow* you.

THE WOMAN (*Snorts*)

Who follows *who!*

THE MAN

Whom.

THE WOMAN

I know: who follows who! Does *she* follow *me?* I don't *know*
anymore; it's so *long.*

THE MAN

How long?

THE WOMAN

I said: I don't *know* anymore.

THE MAN (*Curiously superior*)

Not even how long?

THE WOMAN

Not *even*. It's an old vaudeville act now . . . except not very funny, and . . . thin of reason. Familiar? Familiar territory?

THE MAN (*Chuckles*)

Sort of.

THE WOMAN
(*An exaggerated sigh*)

Oh . . . I should have gone into something else, I suppose.
(*Bright*)

But, then again, so should you!

THE MAN (*Surprised; offended*)

Why!?

THE WOMAN
(*Laughs; parodies him*)

"I do your food; I do your food." Is that a *life*?

THE MAN

I *repeat*.

THE WOMAN (*Quite light about it*)

I mean, we only go through it once. "I do your food." Is that *enough*?

THE MAN (*Tosses it off*)

Oh . . . go slit your throat.

THE WOMAN
(*Considers that; sucks the end of her forefinger.
Matter-of-fact tone*)

I don't think you should say that.

THE MAN (*Quite pleased*)
Does it *bother* you? Does it *get* to you?

THE WOMAN
(*Shakes her head; doesn't indicate the* GIRL)
You never know who's listening.

THE MAN
Who!?
(*Realizes; looks quickly at the* GIRL)
Oh!
(*To the* WOMAN; *sotto voce*)
I'm sorry. Of course! She *does* listen, does she? Or, can? I mean, all the time?

THE WOMAN
Well, you never *know*. You know?
(*Chuckles*)
God, what a language!

THE MAN
(*His attention on the* GIRL *again*)
I assumed she . . . turns off. "Turns off" is how they say, isn't it? I assumed she did *that*. On and off.

THE WOMAN (*Bland*)
On and off; up and down; in and out . . . you mustn't be too sure of anything. We listen when we don't think we are, and sometimes when we think we are we haven't heard a thing. *I've* done it—*both* ways.
(*Overly interested; overly articulated*)
Haven't *you*?

THE MAN (*Tricked into a reply*)
Of course, but . . . oh, go slit your . . . go slit whatever you like.

THE WOMAN (*Shakes her head*)

We must have a *talk* about this; you don't *listen*; *nobody* listens anymore. Why does nobody *listen*? Hm? I told you not to say it and you say it.

(*The* MAN *dismisses her with a gesture*)

What! What does that gesture mean? You, too? Are you turning off, too? Well, what will I be left with? Hm?

(*Exaggerated wringing of hands*)

Oh my, oh my.

(*Normal again*)

Contemplation of . . . what? Contemplation of whether I should or should not slit my whatever. Take my own etcetera in my very hands. Well, it runs in the family—I suppose there's that. My *grand*mother did it—didn't slit her throat, but did herself in, quite nicely . . . and on purpose, too!

THE MAN

(*Interested in spite of himself*)

Really?

THE WOMAN

Really! Poisoned herself.

THE MAN

No!

THE WOMAN (*Feigning surprise*)

Oh, I thought she *did*.

THE GIRL (*A whine*)

Me!

THE WOMAN (*To the* GIRL)

Oh, be still, you!

(*The* GIRL *makes a quick, startled sound; withdraws into herself. To the* MAN)

The event I am about to describe is the day her husband vanished—my grandfather that would be, the day he disappeared. He was over seventy—can you follow?

THE MAN (*Impatient; testy*)

Yes yes!

THE WOMAN (*Not to be rushed*)

He was over seventy, and I *think* they'd been happy—though it was a generation wouldn't let you know, you know?—and one fine day he simply disappeared, didn't pack a bag, or act funny beforehand, simply said he was going into town to get some snuff, my grandmother used to tell it—snuff, for God's sake!—and off he went, and do you think he came back? He did not! Never came back? The man at the tobacco store where they sold the snuff said no, he'd not come in, when they asked, and you can be sure they did; and *one* man said he'd seen him take a left at the library, and a policeman said no, *he'd* seen him go off down Willow past the hardware store; and Mrs. Remsen—the Lord rest her soul—said *that* wasn't true at all, that he'd said good day to *her* at the corner of Pocket and Dunder and sauntered off in the direction of the bank—to which, of course, it turned out he had not been. And so my grandmother made a map—being that way, you know: a methodical family—and found the locus where they all had seen him, some others, too, and determined from that, from all the information they'd put together, that from that *spot*, the *locus*, he had gone off in several directions at the same time. He had, in effect . . . dispersed.

THE MAN (*Puzzled*)

He didn't come back? Ever?

THE WOMAN (*Quite miffed*)

He did not!

THE MAN (*Not quite believing*)
And so your *grand*mother took *poison*.

THE WOMAN
O, ye of little faith! She waited for him—being a proper lady, and nearly seventy, herself, at that, she waited for him for seven years, which is the legal time—or was—and when he had not come back by then . . .

THE MAN
(*Finishing it for her; considerable disbelief*)
. . . she went upstairs and poisoned herself, having put a vial away some time before, to have for some such occasion, being a proper lady.

THE WOMAN
That is what we believe.

THE MAN (*Considers it; then*)
No.

THE WOMAN (*Eyes narrowing*)
How do you know she went upstairs?

THE MAN
What!?

THE WOMAN
How do you know she went upstairs? You said . . . and then she went upstairs and poisoned herself. How do you know she went upstairs? That's very suspicious.

THE MAN
(*Unable to believe the discussion*)
I *didn't* know! I assumed it! It's a phrase—she went upstairs and poisoned herself.

THE GIRL (*Plaintive*)
Me? Please?

THE WOMAN (*To the* GIRL)
No! Me! You wait your turn!

THE GIRL (*A whine*)
When?

THE WOMAN
Eventually.

THE VOICE
Fifteen.

THE WOMAN
(*The* GIRL *subsides as before. To the* MAN)
She said—my grandmother, and my mother would verify it if
she were still alive, for she was there in the room with me,
and I was very little—she said, my grandmother did— "It's
seven years today, do you realize that? Seven years to the day.
Clearly he's dead." She stood up then and went to the stair—
and I remember her hand on the newel post, so well: delicate,
withered hand, with liver spots—and she stood there by the
stair, and she said, so evenly, so softly, "He's dead; clearly
he's dead. I shouldn't think I'd enjoy it much without him,
not after all this time." She turned then; she lifted her long
skirt gently and went upstairs to her room—a light woman,
all bones.
(*Pause*)
When we called her for dinner and she didn't come, we went
up to her, my mother and I—she holding on to me, my hand,
I was so little—we went in her room, calling first, then knock-
ing, and there she was, on her bed, quite properly, long dress
neat, fingers twined. She was dead.
(*Simply; to explain dogma*)
He died; so did she.

THE MAN (*Dry*)

One assumption, one fact.

THE WOMAN (SHE, *too*)

Be that as it may.

THE MAN
(*A tinge of disrespect*)

Very touching.

THE WOMAN (*Nailing it down*)

He died; and so did she.

THE MAN (*Considerable disbelief*)

By poisoning herself.

THE WOMAN (*Above it*)

That is what we believe.

THE MAN

I dare say.

THE WOMAN (*Smiles, remembers*)

She said to me once, not long before she died, when I was
just old enough to make sense of what I heard, she said, "We
don't have to live, you know, unless we wish to; the greatest
sin, no matter what they *tell* you, the greatest sin in living is
doing it badly—stupidly, or as if you weren't really alive, *or*
wickedly; taking it in your own hands, taking your life in your
own two hands may be the one thing you'll ever do in the
whole stretch that matters."

THE MAN
(*Shakes his head in mock amazement*)

You remember all that, every comma; and you so little.

THE WOMAN
(*Opens her mouth, shuts it; opens it again*)
You're not very nice.

THE MAN (*An imitation*)
Who's *nice?*
(THEY BOTH *chuckle ruefully*)

THE GIRL (*Very plaintive; a child*)
Me? Me, now? Please?

THE WOMAN (*Sing-song; to a baby*)
No, no; not now.

THE GIRL
Please? Me?

THE WOMAN (*Sighs heavily*)
All right. You.

THE GIRL (*Shy; tentative*)
Start me? Please?

THE WOMAN
With a snap? Like this?
(SHE *snaps her fingers*)

THE VOICE
Sixteen.

THE GIRL
(*More tentative, stumbling than usual*)
You . . . you don't listen.

THE WOMAN
Well, that may *be.*

THE GIRL

Pay, pay . . . pay attention, rather, is what you don't do.
Cry: you say she cried!

THE WOMAN (*Her mind elsewhere*)

Who? The girl you hit?

THE GIRL (*Shrill*)

Certainly!

THE WOMAN (*Not too involved*)

Yes; she cried.

THE GIRL
(*Great, quiet intensity; a hissing quality*)

What do *you* know about crying? Did you ever see *me* cry?
Has *he* ever cried? How do you *know* she was crying?

THE WOMAN (*An abrupt laugh*)

That's quite a list.
(*A barker*)

The answers, ladies and gentlemen, are . . . plenty . . . yes,
I *think* so . . . yes, he has . . . *and* . . . tears were coming
from her eyes, there were sounds in her throat, and there was
no joy in her heart.

THE MAN (*Sadly ironic*)

Have you? Within memory? *Have* you cried?

THE WOMAN

Well, I'm not a blubberer, like *some*.

THE GIRL
(*High-pitched; close to hysteria*)

There was no joy in her heart?

THE MAN
(*Answering the* WOMAN; *a sad, quiet truth*)
The only people who can show it are those who have it.

THE WOMAN (*Smiles*)
No cod piece for the psyche, eh?

THE GIRL (*Even more insistent*)
There was no joy in her heart?

THE WOMAN
(*Swings on the* GIRL; *cold*)
No; no joy! Do you know why she was sitting there beside
you that day? Hm? Do you know why she was *there?!*

THE GIRL
(*Knowingly inventing a wrong answer*)
Of course: to steal!

THE WOMAN
Or to be hit? *You* know better.

THE GIRL (*Transparent*)
No.

THE WOMAN
(*Thinks for a moment*)
Well, maybe conscious lies are an improvement; they'll be
interested in that. I must bring it *up.*
(*Harsh*)
Do you *want* to know why she was there?!

THE GIRL (*Totally ambiguous*)
Don't be silly.

THE WOMAN (*Pressing*)

She was there because she was at home one day—her sister tells it—around three in the afternoon, a September day, the weekend before them, her husband coming in on the train, when she folded her hands, pursed her lips and said, "Reality is too *little* for me."

(*Pause*)

THE MAN (*Quietly*)

Well, *that's* a switch.

THE WOMAN (*To the* GIRL)

And so there she was, there beside *you*, things taking their course, and what did *you* do? You *hit* her.

THE GIRL
(*Mild and unconcerned*)

I hit her because she deserved it.
(*Strangely curious*)
She had *those* things? All *those* things?

THE WOMAN

What; which?

THE GIRL (*Shrugs*)

Weekends . . . September . . . reality.

THE WOMAN

Um-hum.

THE GIRL (*Dismissing it*)

Well, we've *all* had that.

THE WOMAN (*Playing her along*)

Oh, yes. *And* a husband, *and* a baby.

THE GIRL (*Knits her brow*)

Well, not all of us that.

THE MAN

I don't think of myself as a blubberer.

THE WOMAN

Oh, was it *you!?* Was I talking about *you?*

THE GIRL

It was three? It was in the afternoon?

THE WOMAN

(*Still gauging the* MAN's *reactions*)

Around three; I have it from the sister; September.

THE GIRL (*So reasonable*)

Well, she could have said she wanted it—the cardboard—that she needed it; she could have had it.

THE WOMAN

And you would have given it to her: "Here you are, sweetie." Now you're a liar on top of everything else.

THE GIRL (*Sudden*)

W*hat* else!?

THE WOMAN

Everything! You're a common liar.

THE GIRL (*Blasé*)

I don't re*member* much, that's all.

THE MAN (*Accusatory*)

Kiss the boys and make them cry? *All* of them? How *many?*

THE WOMAN (*Dismissing him*)

Oh, choose a number.

(*Back to the* GIRL)

No; common or garden variety liar. I thought I *knew* you.

THE GIRL

She had September, did she?

THE WOMAN

(*Looking her straight in the eye*)

A good month, September.

THE GIRL (*Shrugs*)

They *all* have something . . .   I don't care; have it whatever way you want; these people cry or they don't cry; you don't have to *do* anything most of the time. They just cry.

(*Bright*)

Wasn't that good? They just cry.

THE WOMAN

(*Following; tolerating*)

And she didn't cry because you *hit* her.

THE GIRL (*Contemptuous*)

No; she cried *when* I hit her; it took her that long; the tears were over what I had, not what I did.

THE WOMAN

(*Head-shaking, grudging admiration*)

Wow!

THE GIRL (*Quietly superior*)

Everything figures out; you just have to look; pay attention; listen. You *do* do that, don't you?

THE WOMAN (*Steel*)

I try. She was just a little slow, is that it?

THE GIRL (*Pleased*)

Just a little; that's it.

THE WOMAN (*Nailing it down*)

Not *you*, though: quick, if anything, hunh?

THE GIRL

No; yes.

THE WOMAN (*Airy*)

Well, I'll take it up at the next meeting.

THE GIRL (*Challenging*)

You do that.

THE WOMAN

All logical and well thought out; *that* deserves a session by itself; no telling *what* it means; step forward?, step back?

THE GIRL (*Head high*)

Have fun!
(*Becomes private, settles her gaze on the pool. Pause*)

THE MAN

What happened to the baby? You said she had a baby.

THE WOMAN

Who? The September girl? The one this one hit?

THE MAN

Yes.

THE WOMAN (*Quite matter-of-fact*)

September afternoon; she climbed the stair.
(*Laughs*)
Oh, God! "She climbed the stair." She climbed the stair; she took the baby from the crib, she took it by the ankles . . .

THE MAN

No! Please!

THE WOMAN

Took it by its ankles and bashed its head against the wall. I suppose that gained a *little* more reality; *I* don't know.
(*Pause*)
She's a sad girl.

THE GIRL
(*Not looking up; quietly; a pout*)

She took my cardboard, or would have. How can you trust someone climbs the stairs?

THE WOMAN (*Weary*)

Oh, hush!
(*Pause*)

THE VOICE

Seventeen.

THE MAN
(*Shakes his head; determined, if sad*)

I'm *not* a blubberer. I may have been once, and I may well be again . . . but I'm not *now*.

THE WOMAN (*Bright interest*)

Oh?

THE MAN (*A quiet dig*)
How *can* you trust someone climbs the stairs?

THE GIRL (*From "far off"*)
Yes.

THE WOMAN
(*Pointing the* MAN *toward the subject*)
"Blubbering."

THE MAN
The baby by its ankles? Well, that might start me again, or
turn me off for good. I think ankles is the word.

THE WOMAN
Oh?

THE MAN
Mmmm. It's the leverage—swung by the ankles, all that
centrifugal on the way to it, to the wall. It's horrible!

THE WOMAN
Ohhhhhh . . . .

THE MAN
Why are people so *inventive!?*

THE WOMAN
Grow up, will you! You romantics! If I'd told you she put the
baby on the floor and stepped on its head you'd say the same
thing—or pushed it in the toilet. You're a romantic: wars
don't get you; you'd probably *come* in an earthquake . . . .

THE MAN
Be fair!

THE WOMAN (*Cruel*)

Who's fair!?

(*Subsiding*)

Who's nice? Who's anything?

THE MAN (*After a moment; shy*)

I hate that laugh of yours, but in spite of it . . . *you* were fair; *you* were nice; *you* were something.

THE WOMAN

HA!

(*Now a rueful chuckle*)

Well . . . I dare say I *must* have been—something or other. Maybe not fair; maybe not nice; but *some*thing.

THE MAN (*Nods*)

Um'hum.

THE WOMAN

Was I one-of-those-three-take-your-choice?

THE MAN

Um-hum.

THE WOMAN (*Almost coquettish*)

I wonder which one.

THE GIRL (*Stentorian—for her*)

A set of principles. One: you cannot trust someone climbs the stairs.

THE WOMAN

Ignore her.

THE MAN

Is that safe?

THE WOMAN (*Laughs*)

No; nor is paying attention, I begin to think. Don't answer is what I mean. Don't answer *her*. Answer me.

THE MAN

Oh?

THE WOMAN

Yes. Which one?

THE MAN

All three. I *said*.

THE WOMAN (*Very matter-of-fact*)

I don't *believe* it.

THE MAN

Well, that tells you less about how you were than how you are.

THE WOMAN

You never knew me. It was someone else; it was lots of *other* people.

THE MAN (*Smiles*)

I knew things *about* you; I knew *parts* of you.

THE WOMAN (*A sad sneer*)

You're a cook. It was lots of other people.

THE MAN

What were they?

THE WOMAN

You're a cook.

THE MAN (*A rather triste listing*)

I knew the things you liked—and I knew the things you pretended not to like, a longer list, by the way. Physical things, *and* ideas. I knew the phases of you.

THE WOMAN (*Precise distaste*)

An "institutional cook."

THE MAN

I knew your losses—even *then*; your prides and your losses. You told me *lots* of things.

THE WOMAN

It was lots of *other* people told you things; I told things to *other* people. I never knew *you*.

THE MAN

I knew which flowers you preferred; you told me all about your father's whip, and all about the day you were strong enough to take it from him, and how you beat him for an hour . . . .

THE WOMAN

(*Curiously unconcerned*)

No, I never told you any of that; it was someone else.

THE MAN

Do you *still* not shave beneath your arms?

THE WOMAN (*After a pause*)

Who *are* you?

THE MAN

You saw me *cry*; remember? You *made* me cry; remember that?

THE WOMAN
(*As if denying everything*)
You're a *cook*.

THE MAN
I knew the things you liked, I knew which flowers you preferred, I knew your thighs.

THE WOMAN
(*Distressed, almost shocked*)
Please!

THE MAN
The . . . hot moist suffocating center of your temporal being? How's that?!

THE GIRL
Two: you cannot trust a woman's thighs.

THE MAN
(*To the* GIRL, *but looking straight at the* WOMAN)
Wrong; it's one of the few things you can trust.

THE WOMAN (*A harsh laugh*)
. . . suffocating center of my *what!?*

THE MAN
Temporal being; your temporal being.

THE WOMAN
Goodness! I'd forgotten I *had* one.

THE MAN
A suffocating center?

THE WOMAN (*Laughs nicely*)

No; a temporal being! It's not a *way* you think of things. "*I* have a temporal being." I think I recognize you; I saw you cry once. Once?

THE MAN

Once. How much do you want?

THE WOMAN

I don't remember.

THE MAN
(*Indicates the surrounding area*)

Is any of this familiar?

THE WOMAN (*Laughs*)

What! This!? Where we are!?

THE MAN

Well, as it was—as it may have been, back when it was . . . what? . . . personal, is that it? Back when it was clipped and trained and planned and . . . back *then*.

THE WOMAN (*Shakes her head*)

No.

THE MAN

Did we leave the patio? Remember the sound the footfall made on the stone, even outdoors?

THE WOMAN

No.

THE MAN

And the sudden silence of the grass after all that echoing, through a bower . . .

THE WOMAN

A what?

THE MAN

A bower.

THE WOMAN

No.

THE MAN

It was *full* then.

THE WOMAN
(*Apprehensive; on guard, at least*)

W*hat* was!?

THE GIRL (*Echoing the* WOMAN)

W*hat* was!?

THE MAN (*At the air*)

Nothing.
(*To the woman again*)

You don't remember it.

THE WOMAN

No.

THE MAN

All this—clipped, then, trained, planned . . . and at the end
of it all . . . you: God, or monster? No?

THE WOMAN

No.

THE MAN

"*I'll* show you something," you said.

THE WOMAN

No; I think you're mistaken. You look familiar, though.

THE GIRL

Three: the past is unreliable, as well.

THE WOMAN

No argument there. You *cried*.

THE MAN (*Rue; a slight smile*)

Oh *yes*.

THE WOMAN (*Getting it straight*)

I made you *cry*.

THE GIRL (*Quite bright*)

You made *me* cry.

THE WOMAN

Nah, *you* made *you* cry. You're special.

THE GIRL

Four: no; never mind.

THE MAN (*Triste*)

Do you *want* to know?

THE WOMAN (*A smile*)

How will I know until I know?

THE GIRL

Four: no; never mind.

THE MAN (*Sad smile*)

How do we know what we had until we lose it? How can we know pain without pleasure, and so on?

THE WOMAN

How did I make you cry? No nonsense now; *how* did I make
you cry?

THE MAN

I rose.
(*Stops*)

THE WOMAN
(*Waits a moment; then*)

You rose.

THE MAN

Sorry; I rose . . . I rose from the hot moist suffocating center
of your etcetera . . . I rose—to be exact—I rose my *face* from
the hot moist etcetera of your whatchamacallit, and brought
my face to your face—my hot and moist face—and I opened
my mouth to say to you, but you must have thought I was
going to kiss you, my mouth from your cunt become a cunt,
a cunt descending on your mouth, *yours* on your mouth, you
must have thought I was going to kiss you . . . for you
turned your face away.
(*Long silence*)

THE WOMAN

Well . . . I'm sorry.

THE GIRL

Four: . . . I'm sorry is never enough.

THE WOMAN (*Cuts in; huge*)

BE STILL!! THIS IS NOT THE TIME FOR YOU!!
(*To the* MAN, *though not looking at him*)

I'm sorry . . . I suppose. I don't *know*—whether or not I
am, but I'll say it.

THE MAN
(*Curiously dispassionate*)
Odd, in retrospect: it's such a thing we all want—though we seldom admit it, and when we *do*, only part; we all wish to devour ourselves, enter ourselves, be the subject and object all at once; we all love ourselves and wish we could. I'm surprised you turned away; many don't.

THE WOMAN (*Slightly unpleasant*)
I said I assumed I was sorry.

THE MAN
Well, it mattered to me then. You turned away—*was* it the metaphor?, the sudden confrontation with yourself?—and . . .
(*Laughs*)
and *I* said . . . oh, poor me! . . . what a sad puppy! . . . "I take it," I said, "I take it this is not destined to be one of the great romances."

THE WOMAN
You didn't!
(THEY BOTH *begin to laugh*)

THE MAN
I did; I swear I did!

THE WOMAN
You *take* it?
(*Their laughter grows*)

THE MAN
Yes! I swear!

THE WOMAN
You *take* it?

THE MAN

Yes!

(Their laughter swells)

THE GIRL
(Loud, shrill, over their laughter)
Five: mistrust laughter!

THE WOMAN *(Laughing fully)*

Oh my God!

THE GIRL
Five: mistrust laughter! Mistrust it!

THE WOMAN *(Subsiding)*

Oh, God.

THE MAN *(Subsiding)*

Ah me.

(THEY subside, with brief bursts)

THE GIRL
(When it is quiet; precise, gently)
Mistrust laughter.

THE WOMAN
(Chuckles; dismisses her)
Yes; we heard you.

THE MAN *(To the GIRL)*
Not always; not all laughter; some.

THE GIRL
(Looking into the pool again)
Yes; all; always.

THE WOMAN (*To the* GIRL; *lazy*)

Well . . . as you like.

(*To the* MAN; *bright*)

And did you cry right then?

THE MAN

With my mouth hanging over your neck, a drop on it? No, not then; later; by myself; masturbating. Oh, God, I was young!

THE WOMAN (*After a moment*)

Then, I *didn't* see you cry.

THE MAN

Well, not literally—at least I hope not! But you said to me later, "I'm sorry I made you cry."

THE WOMAN (*Interested; amused*)

Did I? Are you sure? Was it you?

(*Pause*)

THE GIRL

Six.

THE VOICE

Eighteen.

THE WOMAN (*To the* GIRL)

Eighteen, you see? Not six.

THE GIRL (*Confused; tense*)

What!?

THE WOMAN

Eighteen; not six. You don't listen.

THE GIRL

Well, that may be.

THE WOMAN (*Smiling*)

Pay attention, rather, is what you don't do. Listen; oh, yes.

THE GIRL (*Shrill*)

Don't twist me! I'm . . . me!

THE WOMAN

Yes you are.

THE MAN
(*Concluding the subject*)

So . . . you saw me cry. She's *right*, you know:
(*Referring to the* GIRL)

about time—effect comes *after* act, and you knew what I
would do. She's *right*. You saw I would cry; therefore.
(*Shrugs*)

THE GIRL
(*To the* WOMAN; *strained smile*)

You saw *me* cry, too?

THE WOMAN (*Snorts*)

Hunh! The phases of the moon!

THE GIRL

It's important!
(*Louder*)

It's important!!

THE WOMAN (*Some distaste*)

Nobody else; only you!

THE MAN

What!?

THE WOMAN

She bleeds; once a month she bleeds, and she cries: the phases of the moon. God, every woman from the dawn of time . . .

THE GIRL
(*Teeth clenched; intense*)

I am the only one.

THE WOMAN (*Ridiculing her*)

Oh, really.

THE GIRL (*More private*)

The only one.
(*Sudden; like a snake*)
W*hen* did you see me?

THE WOMAN (*Laughs abruptly*)

Hah! Who *doesn't* know! It's down there on the report: she cries at the sight of her own blood.

THE MAN

Like *that?* A condemnation?

THE WOMAN

Well, no; that's *me*.

THE MAN

I mean, who doesn't?

THE WOMAN (*A savoring pause*)

I don't.

THE GIRL

*Every*one does.

THE WOMAN

I don't.
(*Looks at them*)
Goodness, there's so much disbelief in the world.

THE GIRL
(*Quiet dignity; playacting version*)
I had asked you a question.

THE WOMAN (*Very calm*)
(*Pause*)
What was it you wanted to know?

THE GIRL
(*Sad; retreating within herself*)
You don't listen.

THE WOMAN

Well, that may be.

THE GIRL

Why am I the only *one?*

THE WOMAN
(*Briefest sardonic pause*)
Is that the question?

THE MAN

Be nice.

THE WOMAN

Who's *nice?*

(To the GIRL*)*

Is that the question?

THE GIRL

Yes.

THE WOMAN
(Stating it as a subject)
Why are you the only one.

THE GIRL

Yes!

THE WOMAN
Because *every*one is the only one.

THE GIRL

No! *I* am the only one!

THE WOMAN *(Overly patient)*
Yes; you are the only one; everyone is the only one. Nothing
happened before you? Yes? Well, very true. What you see
for the first time is invented by your seeing it? Yes? Well,
very true. *You* are the only one. *He* is the only one. *I* am the
only one. All right?

THE GIRL *(Shy)*
Will I be the last?

THE WOMAN
Since you were the first, you'll be the last; it *follows.*

THE GIRL *(Simple)*
I don't think I can accept that.

THE WOMAN (*Soothing*)

Well . . . you accept so *little*.
(*To the* MAN; *laughs*)
I remember once, when I was in the park . . .

THE GIRL (*More insistent*)

I don't *think* . . . I can *accept* that.

THE WOMAN (*Through her teeth*)

I'm not *interested*.

THE MAN

Be nice.

THE WOMAN

Who's *nice?*

THE GIRL (*Vaguely disoriented*)

What . . . what *would* interest you?

THE WOMAN (*Perverse; smiling*)

Remembering once, when I was in the park.

THE GIRL (*Almost a mumble*)

About me; I mean, about me.

THE MAN

Be nice.

THE WOMAN (*To the* GIRL)

Who's *nice?*

THE GIRL (*Louder*)

About me! What about me!

THE WOMAN (*Almost daring*)

What *about* you!

THE GIRL (*Pouting*)

Nothing; never mind.

THE WOMAN (*Sighs*)

You want to know when I saw you *cry?* Is *that* it?

THE GIRL
(*Great, inflated dignity*)

Nothing . . . is *it*.

THE WOMAN

Do you want to *know?*

THE GIRL (*Indifference*)

I don't *care*.

THE WOMAN

Of course not.

THE GIRL
(*Accusatory and speculative at the same time*)

What would it *take!?*

THE WOMAN (*Smiles*)

Search me.
(*Tiny pause*)
You're good at *not* crying; I've watched *that* a lot.

THE GIRL (*Shakes her head*)

I don't *want* this.

THE WOMAN (*To the* MAN)

Catatonia—as they said in training—is *not* a small country in Europe.

THE GIRL

(*Agitated head movements—searching for something*)

I don't *want* this!

THE WOMAN

(*To the* MAN; *excessively sweet*)

One of the jokes.

(*To the* GIRL)

Oh, yes you are! V*ery* good at it!

THE GIRL

(*Perched on the lip of the fountain pool, shoulders turning every which way*)

I said: I don't *want* any of *this!*

THE WOMAN

(*Eyes closed, a gesturing finger up*)

I saw you . . . *almost* cry—which is as close as we can *come* —one afternoon; now, when *was* it?

THE GIRL (*An adder*)

Piss on you!

THE WOMAN (*Pause*)

Tut.

THE GIRL

Piss on you!

(*Giggles*)

THE WOMAN (*Shrugs*)

Tut.

THE GIRL

Piss piss piss piss!

(*Giggles*)

THE WOMAN
(*Will not be drawn in*)

When *was* it?

THE GIRL (*Venomous*)

On you.

THE WOMAN
(*Laughs; intentionally not looking at the* GIRL)

Of course! It was that afternoon your family . . . *and* your friends . . . and your *dog*, as I recall . . . your grandmother, your mother and your father, your sister and your dog, and a nice boy, and some older lady . . . and they all came parading up, in . . . *three* cars, I think, with one bouquet and two cakes, and ladies magazines . . . do you remember it? Visiting time?

THE GIRL
(*Considerable equilibrium*)

Nothing has happened . . . of any sort . . . to any *one* . . . which you *say*.

THE WOMAN

And wishing will make it so, eh? Trooping up, *all* of 'em . . .
(*Recites, very exaggerated*)

"Somber of countenance, bright of dress . . ." —all save the dog, of course, which yapped a lot and wagged its tail with a great ferocity—all of 'em come to see the praying mantis here.

THE GIRL

Nor ever *will*.

THE WOMAN
(*To the* MAN; *matter-of-fact, but a little sad*)
And she sent them off; wouldn't see them; sent them back.

THE GIRL (*A question in a test*)
What can happen if I won't admit it?

THE WOMAN (*Shrugs*)
Nothing, of course.
(*To the* MAN)
Sent them all packing—yapper, Mademoiselle, ga'ma—whole
bunch of 'em. Who *was* that nice boy?

THE GIRL (*Caught off guard*)
He was . . .
(*Puzzles*)
I don't *know*.
(*Bright, in a cheerless way*)
Besides, it never happened.

THE WOMAN (*Agreeing*)
No. *Such* a nice boy.

THE GIRL (*Remembering*)
Yes; he was.

THE WOMAN (*Very off-hand*)
Did he *betray* you?

THE GIRL (*Shrugs; a little sad*)
Of course.

THE WOMAN (*Gentle, but smiling*)
Good it never happened.

THE GIRL
Yes.
(*Sudden animation, venom*)
Piss on you!

THE WOMAN
She wouldn't see anybody; ever.

THE GIRL
(*Stands abruptly on the rim of the fountain*)
No; nor *will* I.
(SHE *jumps into the fountain bowl, sits;* SHE *looks rather like someone in a bathtub*)

THE MAN
(*To the* WOMAN, *who is gazing at her hands*)
Pardon me.

THE WOMAN (*Still gazing*)
Ever. Hm?

THE MAN
Pardon me; she's jumped into the fountain.

THE WOMAN
(*Before looking; laughs*)
She has!? You've jumped into the fountain!
(*Looks, laughs again*)
You look like someone sitting in a tub; well, you look like *you* sitting in a tub.

THE GIRL
Piss on you!
(*Giggles*)

THE WOMAN

Is it comfortable?

(*No response*)

Do you feel . . . conspicuous?

(*No reply*)

Well, if you find soap, do your neck.

THE GIRL

Piss on you.

(*Does not giggle*)

THE WOMAN

(*To the* GIRL; *great concern*)

Is there anything in there with you?

THE GIRL

You mean, besides the half blue egg, the mouse bones, the feather and a strand of ivy?

THE WOMAN

Whatever it was.

THE GIRL

That was it; that was all; and . . . was it, or wasn't it; I can't remember.

THE WOMAN (*Shrugs*)

Whichever it was.

THE GIRL (*Exact imitation*)

Whichever it was. So, it either *is* there, or is not . . . as am *I*.

THE WOMAN

Oh?

THE GIRL

Certainly!

THE WOMAN (*Weary*)

All right.
                    (*To the* MAN)
And after the silence came—after she'd stopped them all . . .
though they phone now and again, some of them, not the
dog, nor the nice boy—after she'd stopped them all, and the
silence came down, I saw her . . . *al*most cry.

THE GIRL (*Enraged*)

On *you!* On *you!!*
            (SHE *holds on to the edge of the bowl*)

THE WOMAN
        (*Closes her eyes momentarily, reopens them; goes
        on, to the* MAN)
She sat in the silence, puzzled it, and finally figured what it
was—that she'd *done* it, *finally*; she'd rid herself of it all; she'd
made it . . . to that awful plateau.

THE GIRL (*Less intense*)

On *you.*

THE MAN
        (*Holds his hand up to quiet the* GIRL)
Sh!
            (SHE *makes a hurt sound*)
I'm sorry, but . . . sh!

THE WOMAN
        (*Clicks the side of her mouth*)
Well, when I've got 'em, I've got 'em. No one would come
anymore. And that's when she almost cried, almost let it out

—whatever it was: relief? pain? what? I don't *know*. She puffed up; her eyes brimmed; her lips were all aquiver; she turned two shades red, but she held it in, by God!
> *(Snorts)*

Hunh!
> *(Softer; a trifle sad)*

Well, without a soul to hear . . . why shouldn't she?

> THE MAN *(Feels dumb saying it)*

You were there.

> THE WOMAN
> *(Soft, ridiculing laugh)*

Well. That's close enough; *I* don't exist, you know.

> THE GIRL
> *(Hands still on the rim; fingers pressed hard; speaks
> in a loud whisper)*

I don't exist. How can *you* not?

> THE WOMAN *(Pause)*

Well . . . *that* may be.

> THE GIRL *(A whimpering tone)*

I *do* exist.

> THE WOMAN

Well, that may *be*.

> THE GIRL *(A tearful child)*

Which is it?
> *(No reply)*

Which is it?
> *(No reply)*

I didn't *hear* you!

THE WOMAN (*Quite empty*)

I didn't answer you.

(*Pause*)

THE VOICE

Nineteen.

THE MAN

You cry.

THE WOMAN

Hm?

THE MAN

You: you've cried, too.

THE WOMAN
(*Coming back into it; a little too offhand*)

Oh; yes, certainly!

THE MAN (*Clinical*)

When? Over what?

THE WOMAN (*Bravado*)

Oh . . . all the things.

THE MAN (*Waits; then*)

Yes?

THE WOMAN
(*Disappointment, and a degree of self-loathing emerge during the speech*)

I said: all the *things*: I cried when my parents died; I cried when my cats died; I cried when I was fourteen and someone told me I wouldn't live forever, and I cried when I was forty and I *believed* it; you see? all the *things*; I cried the first time I realized someone had lied to me; I cried the first time I realized someone was trying very hard to be very truthful; I cried the first time I had an orgasm, and I *didn't* cry the last time; you see? I told you: all the *things*; I cried when my parents died; I cried when my cats died; I cried when *I* . . . died.

(*Silence*)

THE MAN (*Offended urging*)

Go on!

THE WOMAN (*Furious*)

I told you!

THE MAN (HE, *too*)

There's more!

THE WOMAN

No! There isn't!

THE MAN

Reveal yourself!

THE WOMAN (*Weary intensity*)

There is no revelation *in* me.

THE MAN (*Great intensity*)

I've kept you as an *object*.

THE WOMAN (*Very tired*)

Well . . . stop it. There are no secrets; everything is exactly what you would expect; leave me alone: there's nothing even . . . unusual.

THE MAN (*Sad*)

Why did you turn your face away from me?

THE WOMAN (*Offhand*)

Was it *you?*

THE MAN

Was it because I had no blood on my mouth?

THE WOMAN

(*Thinks about that; chuckles sadly, shaking her head*)

Oh . . . you're not nice.

(*A hand up*)

I *know:* who's *nice?* Hm?

THE VOICE

Twenty.

THE MAN

You like blood? Is it more than . . . *is* there something?

THE WOMAN

(*Laughs, a little uncomfortably*)

No! Of course not!

Blood is another superstition.

THE MAN (*Snorts*)

Really!

THE WOMAN

The sight of blood and we think our insides are coming out; every pin prick is an avalanche; we're carefully put together, you see, with tape—and if we spring a leak the ball game's over, or however they say. Or, is red the color of the soul?

THE MAN

No! Blood is the color of pain!

THE WOMAN

Nonsense!

THE GIRL (*Softly*)

Oh, it is; it really is.

THE MAN

Pain, you see.

THE WOMAN

Yes, but I take pain as a warning, not a punishment; it's information; what's wrong with all you people?

THE MAN (*Quiet irony*)

Much, I dare say.

THE WOMAN

Everything scares us—prolapse, blood, the heartbeat . . .
Why live!?

THE MAN (*Shrugs, smiles*)

Indeed.

THE GIRL (*Softly*)

Indeed.

THE WOMAN (*To the* MAN)

I turned my face away for reasons I no longer remember.

THE MAN (*Overly patient*)

All right.

THE WOMAN

But I'm sure it was neither blood nor hygiene. Most probably . . .

THE MAN

All right!

THE GIRL

All right!

THE WOMAN
(*Closes her eyes for a moment, opens them*)
Most probably . . . well, no; I won't speculate. Not blood, though, certainly. Blood doesn't bother me much. It did once, though! Remember, I was telling you—once in the park, one afternoon when I was in the park, early Spring, a humid day burning off, surprisingly hot and muggy.

THE GIRL
(*Acquiescing to something*)
All right.

THE WOMAN

I'd come in with a book—it was many years ago—in the city—and I'd found a slope I liked—or didn't mind—and I'd lit myself a cigarette—you see? I even smoked!—and I'd set myself to the book, which was . . . I can't recall, the one thing of it all I can't recall, but I'd set myself to it, and was fifteen minutes in when all at once I had a sense of someone—near me, and standing. Nothing unusual in that—nothing for apprehension . . .

THE MAN (*Smiles*)

Not *then*.

THE WOMAN (*Smiles, too*)

No. So I looked up, and there was a girl standing, and being what I am is something like a detective, I knew what to look for, and it was natural to take it all in . . . more than someone else would.

THE MAN

Yes, of course.

THE WOMAN

Something was evidently wrong. Her face was shiny and not too clean, and I saw she had no stockings—which was unusual then—and her hair was pulled back but uncertain, and there was a tightness to the mouth and that . . . wideness of the eyes, and—most extraordinary, in all the mugginess and un-seasonable heat—she had on a huge, oversize, ratty, matted fur coat, pulled tight around her, her hands jammed into deep pockets—fur arms going into fur pockets. Well . . . I knew there was something wrong. "Hello," she said, in that . . . detached voice I have come to know so well, so often. "Hello," I said; "Aren't you warm, in all that?" "What are you doing?" she asked me. The nonsequential is probably the most difficult to adjust to.

THE MAN

Oh?

THE WOMAN

Jigsaw *puzzle* time, *all* the time. "What am I doing? Reading a book and smoking a cigarette. Do you want to know the title . . . or the brand?" "Do you want me to *show* you something?" she said. Well, I knew very well I didn't, and while I can't say for certain that I knew what it was going to be—*exactly*, that is, for a gun was possible, or a dead baby, who knows?—I knew I wasn't going to be surprised—startled, perhaps, but not surprised. "All right; what is it?" And then she slowly drew her hands from the deep fur pockets, palms forward, like this.

(*Demonstrates, very slowly*)

And her hands were all blood, up through the wrists where she'd cut them, and she'd drawn her hands from pockets filled with her blood. "See?" she said.

THE MAN
(*Pause; dismay and disgust equally*)

Oh, God!

THE WOMAN

"See?" she said.

(*Pause. The* GIRL, *who has been preparing the event behind the lip of the fountain, offers her hands over the edge, in the manner of the girl described above. Her hands are covered with blood*)

THE GIRL

Like this?

(*No one notices*)

Please? Like this?

THE MAN
(*Looks over; greater dismay; greater disgust*)

OH! GOD!

THE GIRL (*A small smile*)

Please? Like this?

THE MAN

Oh, my God! Her wrists! She's cut her . . . Oh, God!

(*Pathetic*)

Do something?

THE GIRL
(Shows her palms again)
Like this? Please?

THE WOMAN *(Pause; level)*
Is the blood all over the bottom of the pool now? Are you
sitting in it?

THE GIRL
*(Looks, without moving her hands, looks back, small
smile)*
Yes; all over the pool.

THE WOMAN
Well; you've been at it a while.

THE GIRL
It only stings. I feel *light*headed.

THE MAN *(Helpless; not loud)*
Do something?

THE WOMAN
Well, you should by now.
(To the MAN; *calm)*
What is there to do? Lock the barn door after the horses are
gone?

THE MAN *(Outraged)*
Something!

THE WOMAN *(To the* GIRL*)*
V*ery* lightheaded?

THE GIRL
Very. Done well?

THE WOMAN (*Gently*)

Done beautifully. There *was* something, then.

THE GIRL (A *little faint*)

Pardon?

THE WOMAN

In the pool; there *was* something; or you brought it *with* you.

THE GIRL

Well, one or the other. *You* said you could hear my *pupils* widen; *you* said they *all* make sounds—the chemical thing, the electric thing.

THE WOMAN

Did I?

THE GIRL

Yes, you did.

THE WOMAN

Then it must be *so*.

THE GIRL (*Fainter*)

You said you could hear my pupils widen.

THE WOMAN (*Pause*)

Well . . . I can.

THE GIRL (*Pause*)

Then . . . you don't *listen*.

THE WOMAN (*Long pause*)

I listen.

THE VOICE (*Long pause*)

End.